The Angling Times
BOOK OF THE
WYE

LESLIE BAVERSTOCK

David & Charles

Newton Abbot   London   North Pomfret (Vt)
in association with
ANGLING TIMES

British Library Cataloguing in Publication Data

Baverstock, Leslie
   The Angling Times book of the Wye.
   1. Fishing – England – Wye River
   I. Title
   799.1′ 1′ 094295   SH606

   ISBN 0–7153–8254–3

Photoset by Typesetters (Birmingham) Ltd
and printed in Great Britain
by Biddles Ltd, Guildford, Surrey
for David & Charles (Publishers) Limited
Brunel House Newton Abbot Devon

Published in the United States of America
by David & Charles Inc
North Pomfret Vermont 05053 USA

Contents

Introduction: The River   5

Part 1: Game Fishing
1   Salmon Fishing: A Short History   11
2   The Present Stock of Salmon   15
3   Salmon Fishing in General   22
4   Salmon Fishing: Spinning   25
5   Salmon: Prawn Fishing   54
6   Salmon : Worm Fishing   59
7   Salmon: Fly Fishing   66
8   Trout   81

Part 2: Coarse Fishing
9   Chub   104
10 Dace   117
11 Eels and Elvers   124
12 Grayling   130
13 Perch   135
14 Pike   142
15 Roach   152
16 Shad   160
17 Other Fish   163

Part 3: Where to Fish
18 Salmon and Trout   169
19 Coarse Fish   182
20 Reservoirs and Lakes   190

Photographs courtesy of Angling Times *unless otherwise indicated*

With the Black Mountains in the distance the river meanders through the countryside downstream of Hay-on-Wye (*John Tarlton*)

Introduction: The River

Rising on the eastern slopes of Plynlimon, almost 2,000ft up in mid-Wales, the Wye covers a distance of about 150 miles before it slips quietly into the Severn estuary just south of Chepstow, after the two rivers have travelled almost 400 miles between them in their different courses. This is even more fascinating when we remember that both rivers rise on Plynlimon within a mile or so of each other. As the infant Wye comes off Plynlimon it is joined by the fast, rocky, Tarenig at Pont Rhyd-Galed. The river has already dropped something like 1,000ft in a comparatively short distance and its character is in marked contrast to the middle section of the Wye where there is very little drop in level.

The river now becomes less rocky and by the time it reaches Llangurig, some 6 miles away, it is much less hurried and comparatively wide and in that distance it only drops about 100ft. From Llangurig the Wye falls a further 200ft in its 10 mile journey to Rhayader, the first really important place for the fisherman. True salmon fishing begins below Rhayader at a distance of about 20 miles from the source. A couple of miles below Rhayader, on its journey towards Builth Wells, the Wye is joined by the Elan, the first sizeable tributary. It is in the valley of the Elan that the huge reservoirs were constructed to meet the demands for water from the Midlands. In its course to Builth the river covers some 16 miles and drops another 250ft. Also in this section two other big tributaries enter, the Ithon and the Irfon, close to Builth. After Builth the Wye runs north-east for a short time before making a south-easterly loop to continue down through Erwood and Boughrood and then into a tight loop at Llyswen before curving back around to Glasbury and on to Hay. This is a total distance of 21 miles and the gradient is decreasing with the fall being about 150ft between Builth and Hay.

We are now well and truly into first-rate salmon-fishing water and it is worth mentioning that it was just above Hay on 19 May 1913 that Major Walter de Winton had a day of a lifetime's fishing when he caught 17 spring salmon on fly weighing a total of 313lb. In this area we also have the Edw and Llynfi tributaries, the Llynfi running out of Llangorse Lake.

The river is now much less hurried in its progress and the next 30 miles take it through Whitney and Bredwardine to Hereford, with a drop of only 90ft. The area has some superb salmon pools and it was at Kinnersley on 12 March 1923 that Miss Doreen Davey caught the record Wye salmon. The fish weighed 59½lb, and was 52½in long with a girth of 29in. The fish had been two years in the river and had spent four years in the sea before returning to make Miss Davey's name famous.

The Wye's main tributary, the Lugg, joins the river at Mordiford a few miles below Hereford and we are now following the part of the Wye which many people, quite wrongly, consider to be representative of the whole river. It is 26 miles from Hereford to Ross by water but only 16 by road and the river is generally slow moving and has great meandering curves. In this section it only falls 70ft. Although the river is not so exciting here, it is beautiful and also yields fine salmon. In 1914 at Aramstone, not far above Ross, J. Wyndham-Smith caught a 51lb salmon and, if that was not enough, he caught a 44-pounder on the same day. At Ross the famous Horseshoe Bend is a tourist attraction as the river curves right around beneath the edge of the town before slipping under the fine bridge at Wilton.

A somewhat similar winding course is taken by the Wye as it leaves Ross and heads for Monmouth. Here again it is obvious how much the river winds when we see that the river distance between these two places is 19 miles while by road it is only about 9 miles. About 4 miles below Ross the Wye passes under Kerne Bridge, arguably the loveliest bridge on the river. It was in this area, on the Goodrich and Hill Court waters, that Robert Pashley made many of his incredible catches of salmon. The only tributary in this section is the Garron.

It is 20 miles from Monmouth to the sea and the tide affects the river up to about Brockweir Bridge. At Tintern the banks are high and muddy and there is a considerable rise and fall in the water with the tide. The two main tributaries in this area are the Monnow, at Monmouth, and the Trothy, which joins the Wye not far below Monmouth. Before passing into the estuary the river flows through Chepstow where, at times of very high tide, a rise of more that 40ft has been recorded.

As recently as the nineteenth century it was believed that the tidal waters of the Wye had the ability to cure a bite from a mad dog and the unfortunate sufferers were taken to Chepstow and dipped in the rising tide waters. One of the cases was a girl who was bitten in Monmouth in 1863 and hurriedly taken for the ritual dipping. People proved they were pollution-conscious even in those days by objecting to so much madness being washed out into the river, making the fish unfit to eat.

The tributaries can have a considerable effect on the appearance and sporting prospects of the river. Starting at the head, the Elan is a clear stream running over rock and gravel and the upper Wye itself runs reasonably clear even when in flood.

Sometimes the Irfon comes in dark and peat-coloured and the Ithon can be particularly difficult. It gets its heavy grey colour from loose shale in the Radnor Forest and if this tributary gets into flood in the summer it can sicken the Wye for many miles and for several days. The Lugg comes in 'as red as a fox' when in flood and at such times sporting prospects above and below its mouth can be very different; likewise with both the Monnow and Trothy.

The Wye and its tributaries have about 800 miles of spawning waters although their use varies from year to year according to water conditions. Large numbers of salmon spawn in the main river as well as in the tributaries.

There are five reservoirs in the Elan and Claerwen valleys which were constructed to supply water to Birmingham. Between them these reservoirs hold some 21,800 million gallons. Compensation water is supposed to be discharged at a constant rate throughout the year. There is a considerable amount of disagreement about the effect of this compensation water on the river. Some say it adversely affects the fishing while others, mostly the non-fishing engineers, say it has no effect. The truth probably lies midway between these two polarised opinions. The release of cold reservoir water must have some effect on the river it enters but any effect should wear off as the water gradually mingles quite a long way downstream. Some research has been done on the problem and the results have been published but there are so many unknowns which had to be taken into consideration that the findings must be considered almost valueless. One thing is quite certain: with the demand for water growing all the time and the amount of abstraction increasing, a very careful balance has to be maintained if the natural rhythm and health of the river is not to suffer.

Fortunately, the Wye is a Class 1 river and is virtually unpolluted, less so, in fact, than it was many years ago. When lead mines were working actively in the Rhayader district there was pollution from this source but since then the main culprit has probably been the city of Hereford whose overloaded sewage works killed about 300 salmon in 1947. The problem has since been rectified. There is no doubt that the fish population of a river is a sensitive indicator of the health of the river. The first signs of trouble may be the reduction in numbers or the disappearance of certain fish. We ignore these warnings at our peril. Fortunately there are few large centres of population close to the Wye which might be expected to cause pollution problems.

The Wye can rise and fall quickly, and there are times, as we have seen, when it gets very dirty. The spring floods generally run off quite quickly and clear water soon returns, but during the summer a relatively small swill from the Ithon, Lugg or Monnow can spoil fishing and leave the water thick for days. Fortunately the Wye does not have the problem of the fine continuously suspended matter which makes things so difficult on much of the lower Severn. (The middle and lower Wye has a higher proportion of soft bottom as silt is deposited.)

Mink have escaped and become well established on much of the Wye and its tributaries in spite of a bounty of £2 per head offered in an effort to eradicate them. They are certainly found in the Monmouth to Glasbury stretch, and possibly beyond.

During seasons of low water, weed can be a real menace. The main problem comes from water ranunculus and in some shallows the thick long tresses seriously impede the flow of water.

PART 1
GAME FISHING

I
Salmon Fishing: A Short History

The Wye is well known as the finest salmon river for rod fishing in England and Wales but it has not always been so. By about 1860 greed and ignorance had brought the river to its knees and it was all but finished. Several things contributed to this. Firstly there was heavy poaching of spawning fish in the upper reaches. Next came the capture of parr and smolts for selling. These were taken in their thousands by small-meshed net and line, and there is supposed to have been a stall in Hereford market where they were openly on sale. It is known that they were a delicacy in Ross hotels. In addition the owners of the fishing rights in the upper, middle and lower river were at loggerheads and could not agree on measures to protect the fish. But, undoubtedly the most serious threat came from netting which was nothing like the modest, controlled exercise it is today.

In those days salmon were netted not only in the estuary but also in fresh water as far upstream as Hay, almost 100 miles from the mouth of the river. The relentless removal of a great part of the available spawning stock of adult salmon year after year had a disastrous effect on the Wye. This state of affairs could not be allowed to continue and action had to be taken quickly. It is easy for us, with hindsight, to see what happened and to declare, quite rightly, that it should never have been allowed. As previously stated, freshwater netting was the main cause of the trouble. For example, the Miller Brothers, expert Scottish netsmen, obtained a lease for the whole of the Duke of Beaufort's netting rights in tidal waters and the lower parts of the Wye in 1890. This enabled them to net salmon as far upstream as Symonds Yat, about 30 miles from the estuary, and in 1892 they killed 12,000 fish. The activities of these people alone must have decimated the annual breeding stock.

11

A large autumn cock salmon

Fortunately, as often happens at times of crisis, there was a handful of dedicated men who were far-seeing and determined enough to begin taking steps to raise the money needed to rehabilitate the Wye.

The first attempt was in 1862 when the Wye Preservation Society appointed extra river watchers during the spawning season to try and protect the fish that were left. Salmon are always vulnerable to poaching when they are on the shallow spawning grounds but the measure had little real success because it failed to tackle the real problem, which was the ferocious freshwater netting, and this continued.

In 1874 the Wye Preservation Society was reconstituted as the Wye Fisheries Association with the aim of taking up netting rights as they became available. Members raised £9,000 for this work which was becoming essential, when it is realised that at that time rods were catching only a few hundred fish each season instead of the thousands they should have been taking.

In 1901 the Duke of Beaufort sold to the Crown the whole of his fishing rights in the Wye and Bristol Channel for £15,000, with a stipulation that the netting rights be leased to the Wye Fisheries Association. In its turn, the Crown insisted that the Association should only net enough fish to pay expenses and not for profit. From now on with determined and influential men in control the position could only improve.

The Wye Board passed a byelaw in 1902 prohibiting drift netting above Bigsweir Bridge, about 15 miles from the Severn estuary. This was followed by the stopping of all netting by the Wye Fisheries Association to conserve stocks. This was a particularly enlightened act and required a lot of courage. Remember that expenses still had to be paid in spite of their being no income from netting and money was borrowed on the strength of guarantees from members of the Association and the Fishmongers Company. In 1906 the Association resumed netting but in tidal waters only.

Things now really started to improve for the Wye and in 1908 two things happened which put the outcome beyond doubt. A further byelaw was passed prohibiting all netting above Brockweir Bridge, some 10 miles from the mouth of the river. Now the havoc caused by the nets began to work against their owners. They had killed so many salmon that there were very few left and the netting rights fell disastrously in value. This enabled the Board to buy up a lot of them without having to pay much compensation, thus saving a great deal of money. It virtually ended the threat of the nets. In the same year, a Provisional Order was made authorising the levy of a rate on the whole of the fisheries so that a regular income was assured. Complete control of netting passed to the Wye Board of Conservators in 1924 when they bought the last of the netting rights. The total cost was £21,000.

The prime mover behind this lengthy and daunting struggle to achieve the rebirth of the Wye was John Hotchkiss who was chairman of the Conservators from 1900 to 1906 and everyone who now fishes for salmon in the Wye owes him heartfelt thanks.

A Great Fisherman and Some Big Salmon

It is inevitable that tales of fine fishermen and monster salmon should appear about a river like the Wye; it would be incredible if they did not. However, there are two remarkable stories about one Wye fisherman and one Wye salmon, not connected, which have been well documented and must be mentioned.

The most famous fisherman produced by the Wye is undoubtedly Robert Pashley. Highly skilled with bait and fly, Pashley made some tremendous catches. He knew exactly where to find his fish and to make certain that he covered them in a proper manner he would often fish across one half, or even less, of a pool, then start again and cover the rest. It was well known that he disliked the highly varnished finish of new minnows and he would carry around a pocketful for some time, turning them around with his hand to dull them, before he considered them really fit for use. His great catches of large salmon, made mostly on the Goodrich and Hill Court waters below Ross, culminated in a bag of 678 fish in 1936. The total weight of the salmon was 10,882lb and the average weight was 16lb. In his angling career he also caught at least 14 salmon weighing over 40lb. Quite a man!

We have already seen that the record rod-caught salmon for the Wye weighed 59½lb but this is not the biggest fish found in the river. A fine fish of 63½lb was caught by the Miller Brothers in a net at Llandogo on the lower river in 1895. But even this fish pales into insignificance against the one found dead by a poacher in 1920. He measured it and sent some scales to J. Arthur Hutton, of scale-reading fame. The fish was 59½in long and had a girth of 33in. The scales disclosed that the salmon had been five years in the sea and it was Hutton's considered opinion that the salmon must have weighed more than 60lb, probably more than 70lb and possibly over 80lb. Naturally, tremendous interest was aroused by this story and although someone had pushed the fish back into the water and it had been carried away it was eventually rediscovered in a badly decomposed state below Hampton Bishop and photographed. It certainly was a monster.

2
The Present Stock of Salmon

We have already seen that at the end of the last century the very existence of the Wye as a salmon river was in doubt, due mainly to the netting of many thousands of fish in the river itself. It took a long time to repair the damage and restore the Wye as the best salmon river in England and Wales and even now we get occasional scares. It only needs a bad patch in a season or a poor run of grilse for voices to be raised claiming that the Wye is finished. This criticism is mostly unfounded, although 1979 proved to be a disastrous year. The husbanding of the fishery resources of a river is an extremely complex business not made any easier by the fact that some of the difficulties are quite beyond the control of those trying to do the work.

Short-term human greed is probably the biggest threat to the Wye as it is to so many other game rivers. Having survived the onslaught of fresh-water netting almost 100 years ago, the Atlantic salmon, in general, now faces similar attack from commercial netting in the sea. When we think of what is happening and the way modern netting methods and locating equipment increase the toll, it is a wonder that there are any salmon left to come back to the rivers to breed. Unfortunately that particular problem has to be settled by international control and we all know how unreliable that is. Netting on the Wye itself is controlled by the Wye River Division of the Welsh National Water Development Authority and there are four methods of taking fish. The stop net is a large purse-type net operated from a boat by one man and raised quickly when a fish is felt to strike it. The tuck net, also operated from a boat, but by two men, is a form of drift net and it is used in the estuary. The lave net is like a very large version of a shrimp net and it is used to take salmon in the shallow waters and pools on the sands.

Finally, the putchers, called fixed engines, are long cone-shaped baskets set in semi-permanent ranks in areas where fish are expected to run.

The stop nets and tuck nets are the most successful of the four methods of taking salmon and the stop nets account for something like 60 per cent of the present catch. The stop nets operate in the Wye estuary itself and are basically of a very ancient design. Two long poles, anything up to 18ft, come to a point with the purse net hanging beneath them. The ends attached to the net are lowered into the water with the boat across the current and when a fish strikes the poles are levered quickly up to secure the fish. The net will, of course, take other fish as well and it can be annoying for the fishermen if there happens to be a run of shad at the time the net is being worked. A few sea-trout are also taken but the numbers of these fish in the Wye are small.

The tuck net has a maximum length of 400yd which, again, is worked from a boat, this time by two men. The method is used only in the estuary of the Severn below the mouth of the Wye. The maximum permitted depth of the net is 10ft, but the nets fished at present are 14 meshes deep; that is about 7ft. There are occasions when the full length of the net cannot be used because of weather or water conditions.

The main drift for these nets is called the Charston Drift which starts from St Tecla's Chapel, below Beachley, and continues down-stream for about a mile to a point just above the lighthouse on Charston Sands. The nets are laid approximately at the point where the Severn and Wye tides merge and roughen the water towards the Wye shore. The spring tides are big and fierce and the place where the two tides meet changes. It should be added that working conditions for the netsmen in the estuary can be very difficult and dangerous and it is no job for a novice.

When using these nets it is found that most of the fish are caught in the top two feet or so but in the deeper waters many salmon must escape below the nets. Interestingly, the nets could, legally, be made up to 10ft deep but repeated trials over many years have proved that a much shallower net is best. The present depth of about 7ft is the most that can be worked in some places because of the shallow water and silting in the estuary. A deeper net in these places becomes unworkable. The nets take about one

Boat fishing for salmon near Tintern (*John Tarlton*)

fish for every five taken by the rods and the whole business of netting is now properly controlled to take a reasonable proportion of salmon entering the estuary without in any way endangering the stock of fish.

The old fishing weirs on the Wye have been gone for hundreds of years and, generally speaking, salmon now have free passage up the main river and most of the tributaries. They still cannot get more than about a mile up the Monnow where a weir stops their progress. There are other weirs on the Lugg and Arrow which stop running salmon unless water conditions are perfect.

The Wye system still has some 800 miles of spawning waters available to salmon when water conditions allow. There are plenty of suitable places in the main river above Rhayader. Between Builth and Glasbury there are wide gravel fords and there are more between the mouth of the Lugg and Backney, above Ross. Most of the tributaries carry spawning fish, from the lower Monnow to the Elan and Tarenig, right at the head of the river system.

In a year when water levels are very low a large number of fish will spawn in the main river and the smaller tributaries will have fewer fish in them and those not so far upstream. The best spawning conditions occur when there is sufficient water in the tributaries at the right time to get the salmon spread over as wide an area of suitable spawning ground as possible. This means that there will be plenty of opportunity for the resulting fry to find the food they need. The early stages of development are absolutely vital to the growth of sound, healthy salmon.

Salmon are quite prolific breeders and they need to be. A 15lb hen fish is said to carry about 10,000 eggs and the spawning is carried out in quite shallow water, about 2 to 3ft deep. At this time the parent fish are vulnerable and a lot of them get poached each year. Quite apart from the losses of adult fish before they have had a chance to spawn many of the redds get recut by late spawners and this can reduce the number of eggs which actually hatch. When there are heavy concentrations of fish on the beds, efforts are made to net out some of the late fish and strip them. The eggs are then laid down at the Glasbury hatchery.

Most Wye fish spawn in November and December. The ova

become eyed after 40 to 50 days and hatching takes place after 90 to 120 days, depending on the temperature. The alevins are about an inch long after hatching and they live on the food in their umbilical sacs for several weeks. This means that their 'life-support system' is with them from the start and this is just as well. Things could be very difficult for the tiny creatures if they had to compete immediately with larger fish for their food in the very cold water into which they are likely to hatch. Food is not normally required until March or April but the alevins start to feed just before the sac is finally used up.

As the young salmon grow they are known as parr and these gradually change their trout-like markings for the silvery sheen of smolts, the miniature salmon. Big parr are often seen dropping downstream above Rhayader about mid-August in preparation for shoaling in the following spring. They often start shoaling in places like Erwood, Glasbury, Hay, Builth and Whitney and they migrate to the sea normally at the start of the third year. This timing can vary considerably.

From the time they hatch the tiny creatures are fair game to almost any fish and large numbers perish at this stage. As soon as they get to the parr stage they become greedy feeders who fall foul of the fisherman who may find it difficult to avoid them. The toll continues as the smolts make their way seawards where seagulls then take their share. Once in the sea the smolts are hammered again before the survivors reach a size and strength which makes them less vulnerable to attack. It is amazing how resilient the salmon must be to all its normal dangers. Quite apart from the slaughter which they undergo in fresh water it has been estimated that losses in the sea can be of the order of 90 per cent. The remaining salmon come back to the river a few years later to continue the process of maintaining the species. Some artificial stocking is carried out and unfed fry are planted in places like How Caple Brook and Mork Brook.

Many years of careful scale reading of Wye salmon are helping to build up an accurate picture of the classes of fish which are found in the river. In earlier days the classes were decided by weight but this was not always accurate and scale reading provides the only true method of classification. On the Wye, fish are classed as follows:

A grilse has had 1 sea winter plus.
A small spring salmon has had 2 sea winters.
A small summer salmon has had 2 sea winters plus.
A large spring salmon has had 3 sea winters.
A large summer salmon has had 3 sea winters plus.
A very large spring salmon has had 4 or more sea winters.

For very many years the great strength of the Wye has been its early run of really big spring fish and summer runs of grilse. The fish in these categories are still there but the weight of the big fish does seem to be falling over the years. If we look at the average weight over a long period the figures work out as follows:

1945–1955	average weight of rod-caught fish				15.2lb
1955–1965	,,	,,	,,	,,	,, 14.07lb
1965–1975	,,	,,	,,	,,	,, 13lb (approx)
1967–1977	,,	,,	,,	,,	,, 12.7lb

As I said at the start, some of the factors involved in maintaining the stock of salmon are beyond the control of anyone and these include what happens to fish in the sea and what the water conditions are in the river during the season. Some years a really good start with big spring fish will slump into an indifferent summer with a poor grilse run, at least while the fishing season lasts. Often the fish run the river later to spawn so they are present, but not at the right time. Again, a bad start to the season can be compensated by a fine grilse run. Of course when this happens the average weight of fish caught inevitably suffers.

The Wye has also suffered badly, as did other rivers, from the ravages of UDN (Ulcerative Dermal Necrosis), the dreadful fish disease which first appeared in the Wye in 1968. In that year well over 2,800 fish died from the disease. It does not appear to be a modern disease because there was a similar outbreak many years ago when many thousands of fish died. Yet after ten years of the present disease it is still a mystery. Despite some research the causes are not really known and there is no treatment. Fortunately, nature is dealing with the problem, and after a period of about ten years the danger to the stock of fish now seems to be on the wane. Although UDN still occurs in the Wye, annual losses are now only a fraction of what they were in the early years and the crisis has passed.

Poaching is still with us and it is impossible to say exactly how many fish are taken each year, but some years a lot of fish are lost. It is not the lone local after an odd fish who causes the trouble but the organised gangs which descend on the river. These people will use any method to take fish with no thought for the damage they are doing and poison and explosives are used as well as the gaff. Fortunately, and long overdue, the courts are beginning to impose much stiffer penalties on the offenders when they are apprehended. The job is a difficult one for the bailiffs who often know who is responsible but are unable to catch them in the act. Even when caught red-handed there have been numerous cases of physical assault on the bailiffs as the poachers attempt to escape.

As far as the Wye is concerned the overall will to preserve the river is there but problems still exist between the land-drainage work and fishery needs. There is little food for fry at the head of the Tarenig where old lead workings are found. These can cause a lot of problems when disturbed and they can poison the water. Again, near the Tarenig, very efficient land drainage appears to have caused the scouring of masses of gravel in the river.

In the future, water abstraction is likely to be one of the major threats to the salmon population and this is something which will have to be closely monitored as the requests for water come in. Hopefully, in a supposedly enlightened age, the true amenity value of the Wye and its fisheries will have to be taken seriously into account when the cumulative effects of increased abstraction and better drainage systems are being dealt with. This is one of the main ways of assuring that the Wye will, in future years, retain its position as the best salmon river in England and Wales. The price is constant vigilance and the close questioning of what the experts tell us.

3
Salmon Fishing in General

Once Christmas is over the dedicated salmon fisherman who has access to the Wye can begin to take a serious interest in the prospects for the new season. 26 January is Opening Day and this makes the Wye the earliest river to start salmon fishing in England and Wales.

Having said that, it would be very unwise to imagine that you are going to arrive on the river bank on 26 January and immediately start catching salmon. Odd fish are usually caught on Opening Day or soon after and these have a scarcity value and fetch rather silly prices. Catching a salmon on Opening Day places the angler in the same rather special position as the man who catches a salmon of over 30lb. Even on the Wye neither of these things happens very often. It should be added that outstanding angling skill has little to do with the achievement of either of these goals. An Opening-Day salmon or a 35-pounder is just as likely to take the bait of a complete novice as it is to be hooked by an expert. As the season progresses the Wye offers every opportunity for the use of virtually all the accepted salmon-fishing techniques. The only one which does not seem to work is dry fly, but that could hardly be called an accepted method.

Heavy water before the start of the season often means that the few fresh fish in the river get well spread over the different beats. The odds on catching an early fish are likely to be more even in different areas at such times. New salmon certainly enter the river before the start of the season but they seldom show themselves generally moving slowly and quietly through the pools. This is not always so for I shall never forget the excitement I experienced one clear-blue-skied Christmas morning when walking the river bank at Goodrich. I happened to look at the river close to my own side just at the moment when a magnificent 30lb-plus salmon slid quietly out of the water,

Salmon angler and gillie on the famous Vanstone Pool (*John Tarlton*)

humped its back and vanished beneath the surface with barely a ripple. That is the kind of experience that makes you particularly anxious to make an early start at salmon fishing. Spinning is undoubtedly the most widely-used method on the Wye particularly during the early part of the year. There are a few enthusiasts who will fish a large sunk fly very early in the year but the method does not produce many fish. There are also many

23

places, where the river is broad and sluggish, where fly fishing is not practical. Generalisations seem to be inevitable and while there are many superb fly stretches in all parts of the river the method is more applicable to the waters above Hereford. As we go further upstream the river gets smaller and rockier and we can cover the fish just as easily, and in some cases more easily, with a fly than with a spinning bait.

Prawn and worm are used frequently on the Wye, the worm being best suited to the gutters and channels of the upper river. During the summer, weed can be a serious problem to all sorts of fishing and in a really bad year, with long periods of continuous low water, it can bring salmon fishing to a virtual halt in places. Things improve after a good flood.

During spells of low water, the river below Ross may fish quite well with fish packing into the pools and waiting for fresh water. During high water the reverse can happen and the lower beats have to watch the fish racing through to settle in the upper beats.

The drainage system of the Wye covers a very large area and the water flows through different types of soil. The result is that, depending where you are fishing, heavy rain can produce red, grey, or dark, peaty floods in the main river. In the upper reaches the water is generally fairly clear when high.

The effects of winter and spring floods run off fairly quickly even after a big flood. However, in the summer the colour that comes in to the river from the tributaries seems to remain much longer. This can upset the fishing for well over a week even though the water level may never be very high. At such times the river looks absolutely filthy and fishing is seldom productive. The ideal arrangement is to arrive at the river in March or April when the first spates of heavy water have gone leaving the river an exquisite clear green. At such times I can think of nowhere I would rather be than on the banks of the Wye.

Incidentally, it is worth knowing that a gauging station can be telephoned on Hereford 55333 for a pre-recorded message on river conditions and prospects.

4
Salmon Fishing: Spinning

Equipment

The most popular outfit for Wye salmon spinning is a 9ft 6in split-cane, hollow-glass or carbon-fibre rod with a multiplying reel. Carbon-fibre rods are being used in increasing numbers but there are some reports of these rods snapping without warning, so they are not yet the complete answer to our needs. They are, of course, light and generally very strong, although they are expensive.

In the early part of the year 100yd of about 16lb monofilament should be attached to a substantial backing to fill the drum. It is a mistake to use too light an outfit for spring fishing on the Wye because there is a good chance of hooking a fish of 20lb or more in weight. At such times it is comforting to know that one's tackle is strong.

On the technical side the multiplying and fixed-spool reels have virtually eliminated 'birds nests' as an integral feature of spinning. In the old days the frequency with which this feature held up spinning was directly proportional to the skill of the angler in using a free-running centrepin reel. Nowadays this particular use of the centrepin is obsolete on the Wye as it is everywhere else. However, in the right hands those reels helped to kill enormous numbers of salmon and once the technique had been mastered the direct sensitive contact with a hooked fish repaid the obvious shortcomings in casting.

My old friend Lionel Sweet of Usk, a fine fisherman and champion caster, sometimes fished the Wye with me, and one spring afternoon he showed me just what he could do with a big free-running reel. It was quite an experience, so elegant and natural in action that I have never forgotten it. Lionel used all the modern equipment as well, of course, but it was with the classic spinning methods and the big salmon fly rod that he was particularly impressive. Sadly, he is now dead but I often think about him particularly when I am on that stretch of the Wye. What an interesting man he was to talk to, and so generous with his knowledge. His death severed another of the rapidly decreasing number of links between old and new methods but, fortunately, there are still plenty of people around who have benefited from his tuition.

The most frequently used bait for spinning on the Wye is undoubtedly the devon minnow. There are now all sorts of exotic American, Scandinavian and European lures on the market but none of them is as consistently successful as the straightforward spinning devon. Basically this is a simple shell of plastic, wood or metal, mounted on a wire flight with a single treble hook and spinning on a bead. The great versatility of the devon lies in the fact that it can be made in an almost endless variety of weights, speed of spin and colouring. I will say more about this later but for the present we will assume that it is a devon which is going to search out the fish for us.

A few ball-bearing swivels, a bait releaser, some Jardine and Wye leads in various sizes, a small carborundum hone and a few minnows and flights just about complete the essential kit. We shall, of course, require a gaff.

Some fishermen use a large fixed-spool reel for all their salmon fishing but the fixed-spool reel comes into its own later in the season. As water levels drop and the water warms up a scaled-down version of the spring outfit is required which will work successfully with a 10 or 12lb line. In some open places a lighter line than this is used when conditions get really difficult but, generally speaking, a 10lb line is light enough.

Technique

It is one thing to arrive on the river bank with a suitable and well-prepared outfit and a very different thing to be able to use that equipment effectively to catch salmon. As I have just mentioned, when speaking about tackle, it is very easy these days to cast a bait with a minimum of skill and effort but there is much more to salmon fishing than that.

The author spinning for salmon on the lower Wye

After a little experience it is a fairly simple matter to understand where trout are lying and can be caught but this is by no means the case with salmon. The most exciting-looking places may seldom, if ever, hold a fish, while perfectly ordinary stretches may have numerous holding areas in them. This is the sort of vital information you have to obtain by some means if you are ever to have more than an occasional success. You will see other fishermen concentrating on a particular part of the beat and this is obviously a help. In addition most salmon fishermen are generous with their knowledge and will put you right on a strange water. River bailiffs too can be helpful and, if there is one, study the fishing map of the beat which will indicate the main pools.

Some preliminary time spent in gaining this information and marking likely places in the mind is time well spent. Most people have neither the time nor the money to spend fishing all the available water on the Wye and they concentrate on a few places. This gives more opportunity for really getting to know water. Once the basic layout of the taking places is known we can start fishing with much more confidence. However, there is one complication. Fish do not necessarily lie in the same taking places throughout the year. Some beats have known spring lies while others always hold fish in the summer. Again, there are pools which are reckoned to be ideal for late season fish. Sometimes these differences are related to the distance from the estuary, but by no means always.

This may all sound rather complicated but it does not take long to sort out provided you know what it is you are trying to discover. There is an added bonus. Once you have caught a salmon in a certain spot at a particular time of year and at a known height of water, the chances are very good that you will find fish there again in other years when the time and conditions are about the same. I suppose it is not much of an exaggeration to say that the knowledge of where and when taking salmon can be found accounts for about 60 per cent of the technique we need. This is never more true than early in the season when few fish are in the river and if we are to catch them we have to pinpoint their positions quite accurately.

Having discovered where the salmon are likely to be lying we are ready to think about making a start. Let's assume that we are using a medium-weight minnow of about 2½in in length. A ballbearing swivel is tied to the line with a tucked blood knot and the length of monofilament below the swivel is adjusted so that the minnow hangs about 2ft 6in below the swivel. It may be a few inches less depending on the strength of the current. In the early part of the year we shall need about 1oz of lead and I prefer the Jardine type which is simply wound on the line immediately above the swivel. Make sure that the metal spirals at each end of the lead have not been left in a very sharp condition when they were made. If the ends are rough, rub them over with a nail file or emery cloth. If the tips of the spiral are left rough they may damage the line. The Jardine leads can easily be bent into an anti-kink shape with the fingers once they are on the line. The Wye leads are made in anti-kink shapes and they have a swivel at one end but they are more difficult to change than the spiral Jardines. If you are using a multiplier reel there is no problem from line kinking as long as the trace swivel absorbs any twist from the spinning minnow.

There are very many places over the fishable length of the Wye where the pools are wide and the current steady and these are ideal for the standard method of fishing a minnow. By far the largest proportion of salmon fishermen fish either from the bank or when wading. Boat fishing, although essential in certain places on the Wye, is comparatively rare.

The basis of spinning for salmon on the Wye is the square cast but there is quite a lot more to it than heaving out the bait and winding it back in. To start with one should adopt a comfortable stance and keep to it with as little alteration in the body position as possible. When using the multiplying reel swing the bait gently around and back the same distance each time. When the rod stops its backward movement note how the minnow and lead move on. This keeps the line nice and taut in the rings and can add yards to a cast. When the rod accelerates into the forward cast try to let the angle of release be the same each time. If you hold the rod in the same grip all the time this is quite easy to achieve.

If this all sounds rather complicated let me assure you that the idea is simply to draw your attention to the very important need to cover every likely yard of water and not to leave enormous gaps in the area searched by the bait. Once the habit of controlled fishing has been learned the delivery of the bait becomes an almost reflex action and is achieved smoothly and accurately virtually every time. It is some consolation to know that if you have fished all day and caught nothing you have, at least, covered the water properly and left nothing to chance. This method of fishing is also energy-saving and therefore less tiring; an important point when fishing some of the large pools.

We shall need to begin fishing some distance above the first lie. The distance will depend on how far out in the river the resting place for salmon is. The further out the salmon are likely to be the further upstream we should move before beginning to cast. If we begin immediately opposite the lie the chances are that the minnow and lead will drop almost immediately above the fish and be whisked away by the current before the salmon gets a chance to see the bait. Such a cast may even scare fish, particularly later on in the season when the water is lower and warmer.

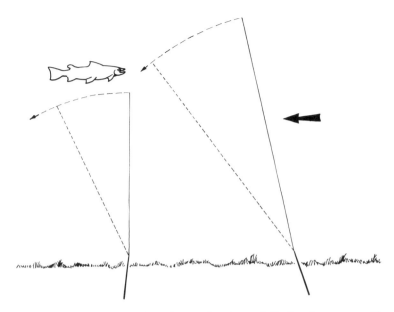

A square cast has placed the bait close to the salmon (*left*). But the current will carry it away before the fish sees it properly. Make the cast well above the suspected lie (*right*) and the bait, thanks to the current, will swing right across the fish's field of vision

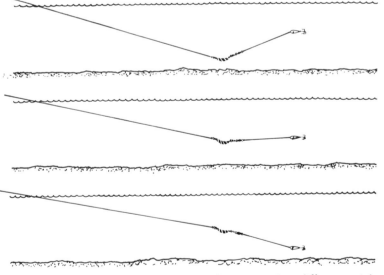

The approximate positions that baits will assume when different weight combinations of lead and bait are used. In fast water a heavier bait is steadier than a light one. In slow water a light bait is more lively

30

As the bait drops into the water give a couple of turns on the reel to take up any slack line and bring you into sensitive contact with what is happening at the end of the line. Once the bait is in the water and starting to fish, try to imagine how it is behaving. It is possible to build up a picture of a lie from your own observations at times of low water and from information other people give you. You want the bait to follow the natural contours of the bottom, dropping down into any troughs and lifting up over rocks or other obstructions. A straight mechanical wind-in is not good enough.

Early in the year fish usually lie in the quieter places in streams and pools in medium to fairly deep water and really close to the bottom. At such times, when the water is at its coldest, salmon are quite lethargic and they will not chase after a bait if it flashes by in the distance. Later in the year, perhaps, but not now. A good lump of lead will quickly get the bait down in the water to where the fish are likely to be lying, but for really effective fishing things are not quite as simple as this. A lot of lead will certainly get the bait well down in the water but the trouble is that if you use too much lead there is a natural tendency to wind faster to ensure that the bait does not foul the bottom. This speeds up the bait and has the opposite effect to the one intended; that is, fishing at the right depth and moving in a leisurely manner.

This is as good a point as any to mention another thing which is of considerable importance when fishing a spinning bait early in the year. Although the bait must move as slowly past the fish as the current will allow, it should spin quickly so a fairly steep pitch to the fins is needed, particularly in sluggish water. It is sometimes said that it is better to have the weight in the lead rather than in the bait as the lead will touch bottom first and warn the fisherman of impending trouble for the bait. There is some truth in this when the bottom is fairly clear but when the bottom is rocky a heavy lead is just as likely to slip into a crevice and become completely wedged as a minnow is, probably more likely.

As in most fishing matters it is unwise to be dogmatic because one's own personal temperament has a lot to do with the effectiveness or otherwise, of any particular method. Some fishermen prefer to know that the bait is going down quickly and almost automatically while others prefer to control depth and movement with rod and reel.

Personally, I like to compromise and I normally fish a medium-weight bait with a medium lead. With a very light bait there is a definite tendency for it to curl back over the trace when casting and this can be particularly troublesome in windy weather. When the bait does curl over, the treble hook has a habit of getting caught in the trace so that the minnow's spin twists everything very badly and the cast is completely wasted.

The medium-weight bait suits my fishing style perfectly. After casting I take a couple of turns on the reel, then follow gently around with the rod point as the bait swings slowly around in the current. Depending on the strength of the current I may not wind any more until the bait is almost below me.

If the water is really deep or, for some reason, an ideal casting position cannot be reached, lead may have to be added to get the bait down in the water as quickly as possible. For all normal fishing I prefer to achieve this by casting slightly upstream or not turning the reel at all after the bait enters the water. Holding the rod point low or high can have a considerable effect on the depth at which the bait fishes, particularly when making short casts or if the bait is directly downstream.

While the square cast is the indispensable tool of the bank fisherman there are times and places where a completely different technique is necessary. In many places the Wye is a very wide river and where the proprietors of a fishery own one bank only, anglers should, in the absence of an agreement between the owners of the opposite banks, fish to the centre line of the river only. When this restriction is in force it is all the more important that the available water should be well fished. In this connection we must remember that there will be places where salmon lie right in close to our own bank. In such places long square casting is counter-productive because the arc made by the long cast comes close in only as the cast is finishing. If it is possible that salmon are lying close in as well as out in the stream it is far better to begin by making rather short casts down and across so that the bait moves more slowly over its narrower arc. By keeping the rod point fairly low and moving the rod from side to side the bait can be made to flutter most attractively right in the area where the fish are believed to be.

It may be necessary to reduce the amount of lead slightly to keep the bait working in this manner without dropping to the bottom and getting snagged. Alternatively, the effect can sometimes be achieved by raising the rod point which, with the rather short amount of line in use, would tend to raise the bait and prevent it fouling the bottom.

When fishing in this oblique downstream manner, avoid pointing the rod directly along the angle of the line. Should a fish take in a heavy manner there will be no spring from the curve of the rod to absorb the shock and a break could well result. In addition, always try to strike sideways when a fish takes below you because this will increase the chances of making a secure hooking. A correctly-fished square cast is excellent for good hooking but it can be very different downstream. Here there is a tendency for fish to be lightly hooked in the front of the mouth and this is seldom as secure as a hold in the scissors.

One of the main reasons why I prefer Jardine leads for salmon spinning is that the depth of water and speed of current can have a considerable effect on the bait. A supply of different weight leads should be readily available so that the amount of weight on the trace can be changed to take account of varying water conditions. I should not hesitate to make several changes when fishing down any of the long Wye pools if I felt I could make my bait fish more effectively by doing so. No one should be slavishly bound by the first weight put on at the start of the day, and a change at the right moment can make fishing easier and more productive. As a rough but fairly accurate guide for bait fishing early in the year, if you never feel the lead touch bottom you are fishing it too high in the water, but if it is continually bumping you should be using a little less lead.

I have mentioned that a light bait has an unfortunate tendency to curl back over the trace, particularly when fishing into the wind. But in spite of this drawback there is one place where it is particularly effective. In the slow deep pools where the current is gentle, even when at winter level, a light bait is much more lively than any other. It flickers and waves most alluringly while a heavier minnow would plod straight on with little to recommend it. Conversely, in faster heavier water a light bait may be far too wayward, tossing about wildly in the current and being altogether too lively for an early fish to get anywhere near it.

A couple of final thoughts about salmon minnows. They are, I believe, like a lot of salmon flies, made to attract the angler more than the fish. Most minnows have a dark back and light belly and the colours are more or less evenly divided. They look very attractive in the hand but look at them carefully when they are spinning. You will see one colour only and that is the lighter one. If you want the bait to really flicker as it comes through a pool, make your own minnows and paint the underneath a light colour not much more than a quarter of an inch wide.

Whatever method of spinning you use you are going to get caught in the bottom of the river from time to time. Once you know the water the snaggings will become less frequent but on a strange beat, particularly if it has a bad bottom, you are likely to be in trouble frequently.

There are some places where a bad snag coincides with a good taking place and one of these I know is still a constant challenge whenever I fish it. There is a deep cleft in a large rock with a two-foot rise of overhanging stone immediately behind it and the bait has to go down into the cleft and up over the rise of stone without hanging about. Too quick and the fish does not see the minnow, too slow and you get caught under the rock. But make the lift at just the right moment and the chances are that a fish will take.

To give one confidence to fish this sort of place properly a good bait releaser is essential. All sorts of releasers are used on the Wye but the most portable and effective is the disc releaser. In fact the releaser can be square or round and it fits comfortably into the pocket so there is no excuse for leaving it in the fishing hut. To make one of these releasers, take a square or circle of wood about 4in across and ¾in thick. Bore a hole in the centre large enough to allow the releaser to pass over the largest type of lead you use but not so large that it also passes over the fins of the minnow. Make as narrow a cut as you can from half-way along one side of the square, or at any point of the circle, to the centre. Fix a piece of strip lead about 1in wide and the depth of the wood on the edge of the releaser either side of the cut. The lead can be nailed on. Then cut a really thick elastic band or strip of elastic and pass it through the centre hole. It is then brought firmly over the edge of the cut and glued to allow the releaser to be slipped on and off the line. The elastic seals the sawcut while the releaser is in the water and prevents it coming off the line. These little releasers present quite a large surface area to the current and exert a considerable force on the line.

They are nearly always effective as long as they can be got out into a good current which will work them out over the bait. But should the bait not come free, walk down below the snag and the current will bring the releaser back along the line to you before you break the line. The most usual cause of trouble on the Wye is rocks and these snags are the ones you can nearly always get off.

The following method has served me well for many years. When the bait gets fast and will not come free by gentle pulling, give plenty of slack line and let the current carry it out in a big loop below the bait. Now haul back really firmly on the rod and wait for a second or two. This puts a small downstream pressure on the line as the loop is pulled against the current and in many places is enough to bring the trace out of trouble. Repeat several times if necessary. If the bait does come free start winding immediately otherwise you may find the freed bait has again dropped to the bottom and lodged itself even more firmly.

If this does not work get well below the snag and apply a directly downstream pull on the line. Again, if the bait comes free wind in quickly. From this position you are almost certain to get caught again if you just leave the bait free in the current.

If the bait is still lodged the releaser will have to be used. It now pays to get well upstream of the bait before putting the releaser on the line. If there is a good bankside current the releaser will move out at once but, if not, you may have to hold the line below the surface of the water to get the gentle flow to bear on the surface of the releaser and take it away. Where the water at the side is really slack you will have to pull off some yards of line and throw the releaser out into the current. Keep the line tight and the releaser will start to work its way down it towards the lead, and it is often at this stage that the bait is released. The final effort is to let the releaser down below the bait by giving slack line, then pulling hard. While you often see fishermen using releasers with rods they do exert a very strong pull and I always like to put the rod somewhere safe and work them by hand.

This may all sound rather complicated but you will be working in a methodical manner and even if you have to go through the whole of the operation it will not take more than a minute or two. With baits and leads being as expensive as they are the time will be well spent. Two final points. After a bait has been released *always* run the fingers down the last couple of yards of line to feel for any roughness caused by rubbing on the rocks. This can considerably weaken the line and the damage is often much more easily traced by touch than sight. If there is any roughness the trace should be changed. It's too late to think about it when a 30-pounder takes the bait and promptly breaks the line. The other thing to do after the release of a bait is to check the hook points. These get blunted and turned on rocks, barbs get damaged and the whole hook can easily get deformed through pulling against a rock. A hook damaged in this manner is useless for holding a strong fish like a salmon.

When a salmon takes a bait really savagely there can be no doubt about what has happened. The rod kicks like a live thing and if the strike sets the hooks properly the fight will be on. However, very often this does not happen and when it comes, the take is no more than a little twitch, just as though a leaf had brushed against the line. These are the takes to be on the look-out for because, until you know what is happening, they may go completely undetected. They are much more likely to occur when fishing across the stream rather than casting down and across and the technique is somewhat similar to that employed by the fly fisherman using the greased line technique. Tightening sideways nearly always hooks the fish soundly.

This reminds me of the capture of my first salmon, a long time ago. The feat did me little credit but it did at least teach me a lesson very early in my salmon fishing career which I have not forgotten. I was spinning a minnow on a long steady stream one spring and the bait was covering the water quite well. I fished right down to the tail of the stream but nothing happened and it

Contact: a salmon is hooked by Alf Bevan on the Nyth at Erwood

was only when I started to reel in that I felt a resistance. Thinking I had got the bait caught in weed I gave a fairly hefty pull—and found I had hooked a salmon. I had noticed absolutely nothing but then I had not been aware of what I should have detected. I realised afterwards that just before I started to reel in there had been a momentary hesitation of the line which had, in fact, been the salmon taking the bait. I learned that lesson well and ever since that day I strike whenever there is anything slightly unusual happening to the bait or line.

Apart from the plucks I have mentioned, salmon will take a bait so gently that the only indication may be the slowing down, speeding up or stopping of the line. If any of these things happens strike and analyse what happened afterwards. In

37

addition, keep those hooks needle-sharp at all times by rubbing gently with a small carborundum hone. I find it best to work towards the bend as this helps to avoid turning the point, which can easily happen if you work towards the point.

That first salmon did more than fool me, it also left my experienced tutor feeling rather silly. The fish played around in a rather lethargic way and although it was below me I had no difficulty, by applying side strain, in getting it out of the stream and into slack water near my own bank. Under normal circumstances this was probably the worst thing I could have done with an unbeaten fish. The water was clear and my colleague could see the fish quite clearly. 'I thought so,' he said, 'It's a kelt', and he grabbed the line, handlined the fish in and beached it. By the time I reached him he was looking at the fish in disbelief. Yes, it was a fresh-run salmon with sealice still on it.

That day's fishing taught me two further lessons. There are times, especially early in the year when fish have just arrived in a pool, when their fighting qualities are not all that exciting. Again, this is a generalisation but it does happen and such fish can be landed quickly. Furthermore, it is by no means always easy to positively and quickly identify a well-mended kelt out of the water let alone in it. The long, lean, hungry-looking creature presents no problems but the others can be a different matter. Usually the rather silvery-white sheen gives them away. The fresh-run early salmon is a steely silver with a dark bluish back and small head and once you have seen the two side by side you will find it much easier to distinguish them. But don't expect kelts always to be emaciated and white; they are not, especially in February or March after a mild winter.

Again, it is said that in the spring salmon always keep to the quiet, deep places, moving into faster water only in the summer. Don't let this fool you. This is one of those generalisations, truthful enough to become a part of fishing folklore. Most salmon certainly are caught in the quieter places early in the year and these places are probably no good in summer. This is because in summer the level drops and the water warms up as the current slows or almost disappears. But in the early part of the year I have often caught Wye salmon well up in a stream where the water, if not white, was moving along at a fair old pace and not very deep. In the first few months you will rarely see fish leaping in the exciting way they do later in the season. This is a good thing because once salmon start to come right out of the water on their tails they become very hard to catch.

Some parts of the Wye have a beautifully clear bottom and provided you can move along the bank, playing a fish is comparatively easy. Sometimes the very fact that there is a great tree stump in a pool provides the conditions salmon like for resting and they may make for it when hooked. If this sort of thing happens where you fish you have to learn to live with it and act accordingly.

When a salmon is hooked there is usually a breathing space of a few seconds before anything much happens and the wise angler will make the most of the time he has, as every second counts. For example, if you are above the fish when it takes, get below it or at least level with it as fast as you can. If you have to run, then run. A fish will often move in the opposite direction from which a strain is applied. If you can keep below the fish and make it fight the rod and the current you will kill it quite quickly. Many fishermen take far too long to kill salmon and the idea of taking a minute for each pound weight of a salmon is ridiculous. About half this time is likely to be more accurate and should be enough on most occasions. The worst thing to do is to try and draw the fish into slack water too quickly, when it still has ample reserves of energy. If you do this and it sees you it will almost certainly rush off to the safety of faster deeper water and the battle will start all over again. Far better to keep the fish out in the current and working hard in its efforts to escape. In addition, any small branches or pieces of wood which come down in the river find their way to the edges of the water and if a fish makes a bolt past one of these it can easily snag the line and cause a break.

Another perilous moment to watch out for when playing a salmon is when the fish jumps. When this is about to happen the line goes slack for a moment or so before the salmon leaves the water and this is the time to drop the rod point. If you don't, the chances are that the fish's weight on the taut line will pull out the hook hold or the fish will hit the line as it drops back into the water.

I had a perfect but very unhappy experience of this near

Erwood. A salmon took my bait very quietly but as I tightened it came almost straight out of the water. It was an enormous great fish, well over 30lb, and only about 15yd away. I dropped the rod point quickly but it was no good. The fish crashed back down on the line and although I was fishing with 18lb line it broke like cotton. This doesn't normally happen and I think it may have had something to do with the fact that I was so close to the fish that, even with the rod point lowered, there was not sufficient give for the line to absorb the shock. The only consolation was that the shell of the light minnow was recovered quite close by, floating in a backwater.

I make sure my kit is always sound and I tend to be hard when playing salmon. It seems to me that the longer you let them wander aimlessly around the more chance there is of the hook coming away. This was vividly demonstrated one day below Monmouth when I was watching someone fishing a sunk fly. He was really in luck because the fish were in the pool and interested in the fly and he could hardly go wrong. But he did. As each fish took the fly he raised the rod point very timidly so that there was hardly any bend in the rod. The fish swam up and down a few times and the hook came away. It was enough to make you cry and I often wonder whether the angler learned anything from that experience. He hooked at least three fish while we were there and was still happily casting away in the same tentative manner when we left.

When you regularly fish a salmon beat you soon learn the best places for landing fish, but if you are on a fishing holiday or take an occasional day on different beats you may overlook this point. It is quite unnerving to get a fish played out and ready for the gaff only to find that you are standing on a high part of the bank with seven or eight feet of water beneath you and no hope of reaching the fish. If this happens, try and take the fish downstream to a spot where you can get at it. It is much less wearing to a hook-hold to draw a fish downstream than to pull it upstream against the current. When you hook a salmon glance quickly around to locate a suitable spot to land it then use every opportunity to guide the fish towards it as the battle proceeds. This will not always work and sometimes a difficult fish will have very definite ideas of its own as to where it intends going.

You then have to improvise and alter your plan from second to second so that when the time arrives you are in a suitable place for landing the fish.

A most useful manoeuvre for dealing with a salmon which gets well below you is 'walking up'. This is exactly what it says and it can save the day, and the fish, when things start to get out of control. A fish is walked up if it is playing in an area which you feel is dangerous to your chances of landing it or if it starts to go downstream and you are unable to follow it because of trees or some other obstruction. Choose a moment when the fish is fairly quiet (not when it is heading full speed for the estuary), hold the line firmly against the rod and hold the rod quite high. Now start walking back upstream, slowly but firmly, and it is odds on that the fish will follow quite meekly. Walk twenty yards or so then walk back towards the spot where you started, reeling up all the time but keeping the line slack. You can repeat this procedure until the fish has been brought into an area where you can more easily dictate how the battle will proceed.

There are only two points to observe to make this technique succeed. First, keep a firm pressure on the fish when walking it up, but don't tug or jerk. Second, in nine cases out of ten the salmon will follow you like a lamb when the pressure is on but, just occasionally, a difficult fish may decide to set off again. What you do in such a case depends on how dangerous a position the fish is in. If there is plenty of room let him go for a while then, when he settles, start walking up again. But if you know that by letting the fish have its head you will lose him you just have to dig your foot in and hold everything tight. Ten or fifteen seconds will decide whether the fish wins or you do.

The best Wye fish I have caught, a fine 35½-pounder responded magnificently to walking up. He made a lovely head-and-tail rise in a good taking place late on a June evening and took my minnow second cast. The fish cruised strongly about for five minutes then shot out of the water and shook itself before hitting the surface again. No problem there. Then it started to drop downstream and with the current to help it, it was really giving me some stick. Fortunately I was using a strong outfit and 16lb line which I knew was in good shape. The crisis came a couple of minutes later when I was unable to follow the fish any further because of trees on the bank. It was a matter of stopping the fish or letting it run out all my line and break me. I held the rod slightly sideways and really leaned back into it. I could feel the fish shaking his head and expected to feel everything go slack at any moment but I was lucky. The fish was well hooked and he eventually rolled on the surface and I knew that, except for an accident, he was mine. I walked him up twice to get back some forty yards of line and found that the crisis had taken all the stuffing out of him. He was on the bank in just seventeen minutes.

Gaffing a salmon is a simple business if it is done properly and it is only a matter of keeping cool and working carefully. I much prefer to gaff my own fish unless I am with someone I know and trust. If you have two inexperienced anglers, one fishing and the other waiting to gaff, you can get into all sorts of trouble. It's very understandable because as he brings the fish in the fisherman will be urging the man with the gaff to get on with it and that is enough to make him flap. When this happens the gaffer is likely to stab at the fish and frighten it or gaff the fish over the line. As long as it is not your own fish it is quite hilarious to see the antics of someone trying to free a gaff from a line as the fish pulls harder and harder to try and escape.

To gaff with a minimum of risk the fish must be well played out. The man with the gaff crouches at the waterside where there is a fair depth of water and the fish is drawn in to him. As the salmon cruises quietly past, the gaff is put out over the dorsal fin. In one movement it is then lowered on to the back of the fish, and pulled in, and in the same movement the pull is turned into a lift. The pull should be quite gentle and should never turn into a snatch or the fish could be badly torn.

To net a fish, sink the net quietly in the water and lift only when the salmon is drawn well over the mesh. Beaching and tailing are other ways of landing salmon but beaching, particularly, requires practice and a shallow shelving rock or gravel area. Having got the fish completely beaten, start to bring it in, preferably from the upstream side so that any current assists the move, and gradually speed up the movement a little as you walk back from the bank. Keep a good strain on and the fish will slide out of the water and can be lifted immediately by tailing. It

A spring salmon of 17lb is expertly gaffed at Builth Wells (*John Tarlton*)

is better to have someone available to do this for you so that the fish is not left dangerously near the water while you run back to deal with it. To tail a salmon, simply pick it up by grasping it around the root of the tail and lift. Keep the little finger of the lifting hand pointing towards the head of the fish. I do not recommend tailing or beaching to anyone until he has seen them demonstrated. Neither would I, out of choice, try to beach a

43

very big fish nor tail a very small salmon, which can slip out of the hand, unless there was no other choice. It is just as well to know a little about some of these problems if you have not come across them before because it is hard if you have to lose a well-earned fish in order to learn.

When fishing early in the season it is difficult to understand how cold it can be until you actually experience it. Salmon fishing in February or March can be a pretty rugged pastime and I have often thought that at this time of year the banks of the Wye must be the coldest place on earth. The main compensation is that the cold does not stop salmon taking a bait and as long as you perservere in a good early pool the rewards are well worth the discomfort. Your bones can ache with the cold and your fingers almost refuse to function as you realise that the droplets of water coming off the line in the rod rings are forming ice. Do wear really warm clothing at this time of year but which still leaves you freedom of movement. Unless it is absolutely essential —do not wade.

Cover the water thoroughly and in known holding places make several casts from one position before moving half a step on down the bank. Overlap the casts and fish the bait deep and slow. You should frequently feel that heartstopping bump which you have to learn to recognise as the lead touching bottom or a taking fish. Unless you are sure strike immediately.

It is quite impossible to be exact about how and where to catch salmon because so much depends on water conditions. In most years the beginning of the season is uncertain and not many fish are caught. By March fishing should be in full swing over much of the river and April and May could be the best months, especially from Hay downstream. But nature has the last word and we have to accept her course, however reluctantly. The lower part of the river should now be fishing very well but if there happens to be a period of prolonged heavy water salmon will travel through these beats to settle further upstream. In such a year the fine lower beats may be useless for many days, completely unfishable because of the heavy water and not holding any fish anyway.

One thing is certain, wherever you are fishing the size of

minnow decreases as the season advances and water temperatures begin to creep up. By April, about a 2in minnow will be the largest needed and many fish will be caught on smaller baits. In my opinion the size is not critical until the summer comes along. Favourite colours are brown and gold, blue and silver and green and yellow. Until the water really begins to fine down and the water temperature reaches 48–50°F (9–10°C) you will not go far wrong by fishing as slow and as deep as possible.

It should be said that until the summer, when fish settle in their lies to await fresh water before moving upstream to spawn, they are not very discerning. Provided the essential condition is observed, that of the bait coming slowly to them, they will take any old thing of a reasonable size. I have some absolutely grotesque homemade minnows which have caught dozens of fish and Robert Pashley, who must have caught more Wye salmon than anyone before or after him, liked battered baits. In addition I find it very hard to be convinced that one particular colour combination is essential to success. What happens is that one fisherman catches a 20-pounder on a blue and silver and the news travels like wildfire. The result is that other fishermen put on a blue and silver and, of course, they catch fish. Don't worry about this sort of thing, just use the colours you have faith in or a bait which you feel spins really well. Once you have lost faith you lose confidence and when you lose confidence you lose concentration. When this happens you do not catch many fish whatever you are using.

Summer salmon are a very different proposition from the naive creatures they were at the start of the season. Now, spread over much of the river as far upstream as Rhayader will be salmon which have had everything in the book thrown at them. Quite a lot of them will have been hooked and lost or pricked and they will be a pretty well-educated lot. Catching these fish is a much more difficult job than taking the early-season salmon and the angler needs skill and a lot of patience if he is to have more than an occasional success.

Tackle should be considerably lighter and fishing must be on a smaller scale altogether. Lines of between 10 and 14lb should cover most situations depending on whether you are fishing the quieter, wider places frequently found from Glasbury downstream or the more turbulent, rocky water which is a feature of the river above Glasbury. Above Glasbury the course of the river soon begins to rise more steeply. There is more space to deal with fish in the wider pools so a lighter line can be used than would be wise in the narrow rocky pools higher upstream. Here a fish may easily drop back with the current and you may find yourself having to do a swift gallop over very dangerous rocks to keep in touch. The answer is to fish as lightly as safety and your own experience will allow.

Many years ago the upper Wye was largely fished with fly only. Among the new generations of anglers there are many who use bait-fishing methods in these upper waters and they now catch a lot of salmon. But some of the small rocky pools do not give enough room for ordinary spinning techniques and the fly remains the most effective and, in my opinion, the most satisfying method of catching salmon.

It is quite interesting to see how the established ideas for fishing the Wye have been infiltrated and changed over the years. Originally it was fly in the upper waters and bait in the lower reaches but the situation is now much more widespread. The fixed-spool reel and development of baits like the Mepps have greatly increased the capabilities of spinning methods and bait fishing is carried on over a much wider area of the Wye. On the other hand, the simplicity of the idea of fly fishing and its deadliness in the right places has not been lost on fishermen on other stretches of the Wye where many of them lose no opportunity to get a fly in the water. Quite apart from technical advancements I think improved communications have a lot to do with this trend. The bottom and top of the river now know what the other is doing almost as soon as it happens. Opportunity also plays a part because a much wider section of the population now has the time and money to enjoy salmon fishing and their different approaches to fishing inevitably bring about modifications in ideas and fashions in fishing.

Few of us are able to spare the time or money to arrive at the water only when conditions are first class for fishing so, if a holiday or day ticket coincide with low, clear summer water, we have to make the best of it. Under these conditions spinning a minnow is not very productive. A small Mepps or wobbling bait give more chance of success but not much more and on a clear bright day with hard brilliant light it is inadvisable to spin at all if the water is suitable for the fly. If you must spin, morning and evening are the best bet, when the light is softer.

At such times the intelligent use of one's surroundings can move the odds a little more in one's favour. The sun does not strike all the river at the same time in the morning neither does it leave it all at the same time at night. This is particularly true where there are trees on the banks or hills nearby which put parts of the river in shadow. This means that if you arrive at the river early enough you can fish the open places first and leave the shaded spots until later on when the sun may still not have risen high enough to reach them.

Similarly in the evenings there will be places on many beats where the sun leaves the water earlier than it does on the rest and the wise angler will make use of this fact and concentrate his efforts on those spots, leaving the still sunlit pools for later on. The upper Wye is particularly good for the use of these tactics but it is surprising how often they can be used in places right down the river where, at first glance, there seems to be no chance of using them. A small fold in the ground or some trees on a ridge can make all the difference.

One of the difficult things about summer salmon is that they tend to cruise around a pool so that it is difficult to pinpoint them. Also they are much more active than they were in the early part of the season and many splashes will be heard as they fall back into the river after leaping. However exciting this may be to the observer on the bank the fact remains that salmon which behave in this manner can be very difficult indeed to catch. There is little point in moving around a lot to cover rising fish unless they show a couple of times in the same place. The chances are that they will immediately move some distance from the place where they land back in the water and by the time you start fishing to cover them they could be twenty or more yards away on their circular cruise. Far better, then, to go on covering the water methodically in the hope that one of the cruising fish will eventually make a mistake.

Under these bad conditions it is perfectly possible to fish for a week or more and never hook a salmon. The fact that fish are not hooked, however, does not mean that they take no notice of the bait. I know of one particular place (this one happens to be near Erwood, although the Wye is full of them) where half a dozen or more salmon are always to be found in summer. They move amongst the big rocks and seldom seem to take the slightest notice of a bait in the barely moving water. But on this particular day the water was very low indeed and I was able to wade well across the river in breast waders towards the area where the fish were cruising. By sheer coincidence the light happened to be just right for me to see quite well into the water ahead. I could see nothing except the rocks under the water until I flicked a little Mepps amongst them, and suddenly a salmon appeared. It came quite close to the bait and followed it before turning aside. This happened two or three times and with different fish although nothing was visible on the surface of the water.

It would be nice to say that I persevered and caught one of those fish but I didn't on that occasion. What did happen was that the experience set me thinking. At least the fish were interested in the bait and could possibly be persuaded or provoked into taking it eventually. Next morning, at about eight o'clock, I crept quietly up the far bank and threw the unweighted Mepps up amongst the huge rocks where I knew the fish should be. Nothing really happened but I thought I saw a dark shape move briefly near the bait. I wound in, waited a few moments, then cast again and started to wind quickly back. I could see the Mepps flickering nicely but suddenly it disappeared and there was a violent pull.

That little fish was only 8lb but it fought like a demon all over the pool. When I eventually gaffed it, it proved to be even redder than I had suspected, but it tasted delicious when eaten later. I got more lasting satisfaction from catching that fish than from the landing of many much better specimens earlier in the year. The reason for my success was probably a combination of several things. The time of day was right, the size of bait was about right, although I think rather on the big side, and the presentation was right. I suspect that what happened was that in the morning the bait came around a rock and the fish saw it suddenly rather than from a distance as it had done on the previous day. I think this finally prompted it to seize the bait.

Low water on the river above Llanstephan suspension bridge (*Graham Swanson*)

During these weeks, when things can be so much against the fisherman, not many fish are caught unless there is a good run of grilse. Spinning is not very productive and although the fly will be kept in constant use on the streams a sunk fly is useless in the sort of place I have just been talking about. But there is hope for the spinning bait if nature plays her part.

During the summer a little swill of fresh water is quite sufficient to get salmon moving through the pools and they no longer require a substantial rise in the level to get them moving as they did earlier in the year. The fresh water will encourage new fish to come into the river from the estuary and salmon already in the river redistribute themselves and drop into new quarters. The shy, nervy, difficult-to-catch fish of the previous low water become someone else's free takers and they are more inclined to take a bait.

Unfortunately, the Wye can be a dirty river at this time and, if the Ithon comes in, the Wye becomes a horrible grey colour which can take a long time to clear. The effects of the Ithon are seen a very long way down the river, depending on how much of a flood there is and the suspended clay of this tributary can greatly reduce salmon fishing for some days. Once the colour begins to fade sport should really pick up and this is especially true of the upper part of the river where the effect of the Ithon is more pronounced.

One of the major problems for the salmon fisherman in the upper river is the possibility of prolonged low water. If it happens serious fishing may be at a standstill for weeks with hardly any salmon being caught. On the other hand a really wet season will see fish racing through the lower beats and packing in to the upper pools. When this happens the area between Hay and Builth really comes into its own.

Lack of water is a serious problem even in the middle and lower reaches of the Wye but not as serious as it is upstream. One of the main causes of trouble will be the lack of fish because they are reluctant to take to the river until fresh water arrives. If fish do probe their way in from the estuary the beats below Ross may fish well until the salmon get stale.

The lower beats do not get things all their own way because there is one thing which makes life particularly difficult for them —weed. As the river runs out of the Black Mountains and slows and widens, conditions become ideal for the long strands of water ranunculus. The slower current means that more sediment gets deposited on the river bed to encourage weed growth and in a really bad year this can prove troublesome as far upstream as Glasbury. But it is further downstream that the worst effects are felt. Below Hereford things can get very bad indeed; for example, at Bridge Sollars and below Wilton Bridge, at Ross, there is sometimes half a mile of weed covering almost the entire river and cutting the flow to a minimum. In these places the problem tends to become a compound one. As the current slows the water releases some of its sediment which helps to strengthen root growth of the weed. The water inevitably gets shallower and this further encourages weed growth.

Salmon are very reluctant to force their way through these barriers and a certain amount of cutting is done to ease the situation. But where the river is wide the task of cutting is a back-breaking one and may result in scouring of the bottom in the places which have been cut when a flood comes. Even more important is the fact that cutting the weed only eases the problem temporarily. Cutting, which is a form of pruning, can actually encourage new growth so the position could be worse in following years. The only real solution seems to be to follow up the long tendrils to the roots at the head and drag them out. I don't know many people who would be prepared to go that far. Apart from the main river, weed can get bad in the lower Lugg and Arrow. The Ithon and Irfon are pretty good but some blanketweed is found in the Monnow.

It is, therefore, fairly easy to understand that in a year of prolonged low water, heavy weed growth can seriously interfere with fishing and in some places bring it to a halt. In addition, when fresh water does come it will break off fragments of weed and the dead pieces which have collected in slack water get washed downstream. This can be a considerable nuisance to fishermen who have to keep cleaning the pieces away from the line and bait. Fortunately these periods do not last long because the fresh water soon clears away the rubbish.

One way to ease things a little when weed is bad is to stop using a conventional spinning bait and change over to a wobbler. These can be very effective and I use them in all sizes from 1¼in to about 2½in. The big ones are reserved for early season fishing. The method of use is similar to the spinning of a minnow but there is lead in the belly of the wobbler and no more lead is usually needed on the trace. About 18in above the bait I put a ball-bearing swivel. A swivel is not really needed as the bait is a non-spinning one but I use a swivel so that I can change to fishing a devon or other spinner with as little wasted time as possible.

An interesting thing about summer salmon and grilse is that they tend to move up out of the pools in the evenings and into the streamy shallow areas. Grilse often favour this type of place at any time of day, however, and they turn up in all sorts of odd places. It is quite possible that, in wading into the water to fish a main stream, your waders could be giving one of these fish the surprise of its life.

Some years the Wye has a good run of grilse. These lovely,

Fishing for salmon at Eardisley, near Hereford (*John Tarlton*)

bright little fish have been in the sea for one full winter only before returning to the river. They are quick, free takers and they revel in taking up positions which an inexperienced angler would dismiss as being of no account.

I remember one July day at Hoarwithy very well. There is a long, fairly deep stream which gets shallow and rough before slipping into the pool below. We used to wade out onto this gravelly shallow before starting to fish the stream below. Anyway, I was spinning a small devon on the long stream above and had had no offer or seen anything rise. I was now just above the rough shallow and, more out of habit than anything else, I continued casting so that the bait came around almost on the stones. It was seized by what turned out to be a lovely grilse of 6lb. I beached that fish on the gravel, went back upstream a short distance and covered the shallow again. Next cast I was into another fish, quick and bright, almost the twin of the first. One more grilse followed, a little larger, and then the sport stopped.

The interesting thing is that those fish were lying in no more than 18in to 2ft of water and it was sheer luck that I put the bait across them at all. As I have said, normally, we waded out onto that part before beginning serious fishing. Grilse are fast takers and in a good year, when the water levels are favourable, they get well distributed over the river and add a new impetus to the summer fishing which tends to get bogged down with stale fish.

As summer lengthens into September fishing conditions throughout the river often show a marked improvement. The water begins to cool, levels start to creep up and the weed decays. Salmon tend to take more freely, almost like they did in May, and although they may not be as beautiful as they were earlier in the year their fighting qualities are undimmed. They will now be more likely to accept our minnows, Mepps, Tobys or wobblers but, where the method can be used I thoroughly recommend the fly. These autumn salmon can provide some very exciting fishing. The old regulations stated that the season for the main river Wye below Llanwrthwl Bridge, which is between Rhayader and Newbridge, finished on 30 September. Above Llanwrthwl Bridge and in the tributaries fishing went on until 25 October. The season for the whole of the river and its tributaries now ends on 17 October.

5
Salmon: Prawn Fishing

Prawns may not be used for salmon fishing in the Wye and tributaries until 15 April and this is a date which is eagerly awaited by many anglers. There is no doubt that, at times, a well-mounted and spun prawn is a deadly bait for salmon throughout the river but there are occasions when exactly the reverse is true. At such times salmon see the bait approaching when it is still a long way off and they will leap in an obviously agitated manner as it approaches or passes them. No one knows why this happens but, when it does, the effect on fish is very unsettling and it may stop them taking any other lure for some time.

The normal spinning outfit with a 9ft 6in rod will do fine for prawning. The prawns themselves should be of medium size and each one should be as perfect as possible with plenty of long whisks and preferably, but not essentially, with a blob of eggs attached. I think it is well worth investing in some of the beautiful Norwegian prawns which good fishmongers can supply. These are expensive but they are the real aristocrats among prawns, complete in every detail and looking as though they could come to life. It can be difficult to find suitable prawns at a moment's notice so it is wise to preserve some when a supply is discovered. The easiest way is to place them in between layers of coarse salt in a wide-necked jar. Alternatively they can be kept in a mixture of glycerine and water. Kept in salt, prawns become very brittle and it is advisable to straighten them with cocktail sticks before preserving them. The brittleness goes after a very short time in water but it will be in the mounting process that most damage is done.

Prawns have to be mounted in as straight a manner as possible for spinning and they will crack quite easily if care is not used to gently unbend salted, unstraightened ones. Prawns in glycerine look more attractive than salted ones but, although I have used them successfully, I am not sure whether or not the glycerine might deter some fish. No doubt most of it gets quickly washed off in the water but when you handle them it quickly becomes obvious that it is quite difficult to remove all traces of the glycerine from your hands, particularly on the riverbank.

For spinning, prawns are mounted on a spear with a plastic vane at the head to make them spin. Two treble hooks are normally used, mounted loosely on wire and attached through the ring at the head of the spear.

To mount the prawn, nip off the tail and, depending on the size of the prawn and mount, one or two tail segments. Then ease the spear into the centre of the exposed tail segment and pass it very gently up through the body straightening the body segment by segment as necessary. When doing this it is very easy to push the spear through the top of the prawn, so be careful. The length of prawn is chosen, or has to be altered if required, to get the farthest hook to sit right up at the head. Don't push the spear too far into the feelers or it will bend on the wire when in use and cause a poor spin, and don't push it too far back or the hook will not be in a good position to secure the fish which nip at the prawn.

The whole business sounds rather complicated and there are certainly several things that can go wrong, but you can tell at once, from the look of the finished bait, whether or not you have got it right. To secure the prawn to the mount I invariably use pink shirring elastic. This is fine and round and enables a lovely even tension to be applied right along the bait with a minimum number of turns. Tie a piece to the ring on the spear before putting on the prawn and leave one end long, for wrapping around the body, and the other end short for tying. Take the long end down the body, holding down the big scales but leaving the legs free, then back up to the head and tie it securely before cutting off the loose ends.

It can be helpful to tie two or three baits before setting off to the river. It takes several minutes to mount a prawn properly and as large chub and pike will hurl themselves on a spinning prawn it can save a lot of valuable fishing time if you have a couple of spare baits in a suitable tin.

Salmon fishing on the Carrots — a well-known beat below Hereford (*John Tarlton*)

As it is April before the prawn can be used, spinning conditions will have altered somewhat. Any very cold water from melting snow in the hills will have gone by now and as water temperatures begin to rise and water levels begin to fall salmon become more active. No longer glued to the bottom they will move quite a distance to take a bait which interests them but it is still advisable to get the lead well down in the water. Although it is a large bait a prawn is light and it will therefore fish higher in the water than all but the very lightest of minnows. It may be necessary to reduce the length of the trace to about 2ft to get the prawn down if the water is on the cold side.

The square cast is excellent for prawn fishing and as long as the bait can be seen to be spinning freely it can be allowed to swing slowly around with barely a touch on the reel. Where possible let the prawn hang in the current below and move the rod from side to side before winding in. This can sometimes make a fish decide to take hold but, if it does, remember to strike

56

in as flat and sideways a manner as you can. This downstream position of a bait can be attractive to salmon but it is certainly the weakest position from which to hook one well.

It is quite incredible how delicately a fish can intercept a prawn and follow and nip it without the angler knowing anything about it until he winds in the bait and finds the white marks on it. I have watched from a bridge while someone was spinning a prawn right beneath me. A salmon rose quietly from below to inspect the bait, fell back downstream at exactly the same speed as the prawn and mouthed it several times. The fisherman saw and felt nothing and hardly believed me when I told him what had happened. The answer in this particular case was to use a much smaller mount and prawn, and fish it a little deeper. It was taken almost at once and the fish was securely hooked. How nice if this happened every time.

You need to fish out each cast thoroughly when prawning and bring the bait right back to you rather than pull it out of the water as quickly as possible. Salmon will follow a prawn right across a pool and although they will follow any bait I think they will follow a prawn more deliberately than anything else. Get into the habit of looking just behind the bait rather than at it when it comes into view and you will occasionally see the dark indistinct shape of a salmon following it. It will take a prawn as it is being lifted from the water and I have more than once had a salmon actually bump into my legs when wading and spinning. If a fish turns away at the last moment give him a little time to return to his lie, then make, as near as possible, the same cast as you made before. This time wind a little faster, right to your feet. It might work.

An alternative method of fishing the prawn is to mount it on a non-spinning flight, add a little lead to the trace and fish the bait almost like a fly. In gentle water the lead can be dispensed with but you will have to get the prawn thoroughly soaked otherwise it will float. I think that the smaller prawns are best for this type of fishing and the method is ideally suited to covering pinpointed fish in suitable lies. The idea is to get above the fish and let down the prawn until it is swinging gently in front of or slightly above his lordship and, hopefully, tormenting him to take. There are good anglers who consider this way of using the prawn much more killing than spinning it and it is certainly more useful in low summer conditions. At this time the answer to the question, 'When should I spin?,' is 'Not at all.' It can do more harm than good and the splash of the lead can be upsetting to fish and the bait itself much too aggressive. On these occasions a light spinning outfit or fly rod can be used to drift a small prawn or shrimp down to dour salmon. A long shanked hook is used to mount a shrimp and as it hangs, just below the surface near the fish, the line can be gently twitched, hopefully to give the bait a little extra interest and attraction.

6
Salmon: Worm Fishing

This can be a very interesting method of catching salmon and there are times when a couple of large lobworms will take a fish when everything else has failed. It is by no means the infallible lure that some people would have you believe and it needs to be used at the right time for the best results. What is the right time is very hard to define but it is usually good in low clear water, with a tinge of colour just before a flood and before salmon begin to move, and again when most of the colour has run off after a flood. Incidentally, worm fishing for salmon is not allowed on the Wye and tributaries between 31 August and 15 April in the following year.

The normal 9ft 6in spinning rod and multiplier reel will do well for worming or even a big fly rod and reel, depending on how far you have to cast. Lobworms may have to be bought if the weather is cold but when things warm up, and especially if the weather is moist, a good supply can be obtained on most lawns or playing fields. The grass has to be short and the worms gathered at night when they come out of their holes. A dark, warm and moist night is best and a powerful torch or lantern is needed. You have to tread quietly and work methodically because some nights the quarry is very jumpy and will shoot back into their holes when the light falls on them. Usually, though, they do not move until you actually touch them.

Initially, it is rather difficult to decide which is the free end of the worm and this is very important. Work the light very close to the feet to avoid alerting worms too far afield and when one is spotted grasp it from above and pin it just where it enters the hole. The worm then has to be eased out of its hole and popped into a large jar or similar container. When you have enough keep them in slightly damp moss and turn the container daily to keep the worms working. This toughens them beautifully and even a few hours in moss makes a lot of difference. Freshly-caught worms tend to be too fragile to stay properly on the hook.

You will also need plenty of good quality eyed hooks, about size 2/0, and lots of drilled bullets of varying weights. A few ordinary sizeable swivels complete the outfit.

The whole question of why salmon take a worm is something which has never been really resolved. It is known that salmon do not normally feed in fresh water and that they live off their stored energy while in the river. Fish caught on the rod do not have food inside them but they do attack our flies, minnows and prawns and I know from personal experience that salmon will take and swallow worms.

Most anglers who use the worm will have experienced this phenomenon but I remember one particular case which was very interesting. It was summer and the water was low and clear and quite warm and conditions were so bad I gave up fly fishing and salmon fishing altogether and decided to have a bit of fun with a worm to see what would come along. I put a couple of fairly large ordinary worms on a little trout-spinning kit, weighted them with a small drilled bullet and tossed the bait out into a fairly slack hole at the edge of the salmon catch. It was quite a relaxing change to sit quietly on the bank looking at the river, watching the line and waiting for the twitches which would tell me that possibly an eel was interested in the bait. Nothing happened for quite a long time, then there were two or three tiny pulls and I got ready to strike. Nothing else happened and it seemed obvious that my eel had decided against taking the bait. In the end I got fed up and thought I would reel in to see whether the bait had been taken. As I raised the little rod and started to reel there was a heavy resistance and as the line began to hiss through the water it quickly became obvious that I was into a salmon. He gave me a testing time on the light kit, it was a 6lb line, but I was in a good clear place and in less than ten minutes I was able to tail a lovely little 8lb salmon. I had seen and felt almost nothing when the fish took the bait but he had got those worms so far down his throat that they had to be cut out and no one will ever convince me that that salmon did not intend to swallow them. It is, of course, a different matter as to what would have happened to the worms had the fish actually managed to swallow them without getting caught. He might have ejected them. I should say that the way the salmon took the worms on this occasion is not the normal way. There is usually much more movement and a more definite pattern.

Anyway, worming for salmon is usually best carried out in the upper parts of the river where it is narrower and you know quite accurately where the fish are lying. The rocky runs and tight pools are ideal for the method and worming is much more suited to these conditions than to the huge, wide pools of the lower river. Also, further downstream there are many more coarse fish which tend to attack the worms and spoil them for the main quarry.

If you do use the worm in the middle or lower parts of the river try and fish it directly to a salmon you know to be resting in a pool or stream rather than attempt to cover a lot of water as you do with a minnow. This is undoubtedly the most productive method of operation, even on the upper waters, so take every opportunity of marking down fish before making a start. Really wary and shy fish which have shunned other lures may come to a well-presented worm.

From May onwards, depending on water conditions, will be the best time to fish the worm and low water summer conditions can be really good. A worm does not normally upset salmon as, for example, a prawn might do and it seems to cause less trouble than even a spun minnow on occasion. Where conditions are right and the pressure of fishing allows, try a fly first, then a minnow or worm and lastly a plug or prawn. If there are several anglers fishing the same beat this may not be possible but I think it is a reasonable pattern to aim for when trying to catch salmon and that, after all, is what we are trying to do.

When worming for salmon I would not willingly go below a 10lb line and frequently use 12 or 14lb. Even with this strength you need to be constantly alert to spot any signs of damage to the line caused by snagging. I put an ordinary swivel about 18in from the hook, depending on the strength of the current and depth of water. The distance may have to be a little less if the current is very strong and possibly a little more in a gently flowing place. If regularly fishing bad places from a snagging point of view I should use a reel line of 14lb and a hook length of 12lb.

Usually it is the lead that gets fast but by no means always.

The bullet or other form of lead, is attached to the top ring of the swivel by a loop of 3lb monofilament to let the lead hang down not more than about 3in at the most. The weight should barely hold bottom and a slight raising of the rod should be enough to move the weight a little downstream. Thread the first lob around the bend of the hook and up the shank and simply hang the second one over the point of the hook. Two worms are enough unless they are not very big, when a third can be added.

Move quietly and as little as possible. Keep well down under the bank and off the skyline because salmon will lie quite close in to the bank and there is no point in alerting them unnecessarily. Swing the bait out gently some yards above the spot where you think the fish is lying. The distance depends largely on the speed of the current and the depth of water but the aim is to get the worms down to the level of the salmon and, moving slowly downstream towards it, not to drop them on the fish's head.

Keep in close contact with the bait by having a fairly taut line but be ready to give slack the instant anything shows an interest in the bait. A take usually comes in the form of plucks or gentle twitching, quite similar to the bite of an eel. This is the crucial time because if you get excited and strike at this stage the chances are that you will find nothing there. Salmon will frequently pick up the end of a worm, drop it and worry it again before properly pouching it and you have to give them time before tightening. The amount of time varies according to the conditions and from fish to fish. Sometimes after only a couple of seconds the fish may start to move away and it is then that you should tighten firmly.

If the fish has seen the bait while moving around the pool it may take it back to its main lie before taking it properly. On the other hand, if you have presented the worms to the fish right in its lie it may not move at all until it feels resistance. Whichever of these is the case the fish will certainly move when you tighten. Often the fish will go upstream but you can never be sure. If you cast the worms square across stream the chances are that the fish will drop downstream with them and you will have to give line until the strike is made.

The method of playing a fish on the worm is the same as when you are spinning and provided the strike has been correctly timed

When worming for salmon tackle losses can be minimised by attaching the necessary weight on a short loop of line. A drilled bullet is ideal and should be attached to a swivel on the main line by a three inch loop of 3lb breaking-strain nylon

the fish should be securely hooked. If the fish does go downstream, try and get below it or at least opposite it where you can exert more control. Remember that once a salmon gets below you, you have its own weight and struggles coupled with the force of the current to contend with and a break can easily happen even with a very heavy line.

The main drawback to worming is the problem of getting caught up frequently. Depending on how you adjust to this problem you either eventually become a resigned but deadly worm fisherman or so cross that you swear never to go worming again. I well recall one session I had near Erwood. The pool had at least half a dozen fish in it and they had all resisted my best efforts with fly, minnow and Mepps. I decided to give the worm a try and soon had a lovely bait ready for action. In they went at the head of the small pool and within five seconds the lead was fast in a rock and the line was hissing in the current, unable to lift the bait off the bottom. I moved below the snag, gave out slack line, pulled and heaved but to no avail. The releaser wouldn't work either and in the end I had to put down the rod, wrap a handkerchief around my hand for protection, and pull until the line broke. Needless to say I lost the hook and the bullet. This happened three times, one after the other and I had got to the stage of remembering words I hoped I had forgotten. On the fourth cast my luck changed and within a few seconds of the bait entering the water a fish was at it and was securely hooked.

When this sort of thing happens you just have to keep on trying. As long as you feel you are not using too much lead for the conditions, you have to persevere. Be prepared to vary the amount of the lead to suit each section of the pool. Two very important points here, learned from bitter experience. First, never keep pulling and heaving away with the rod to try and free a bait. Second, get the releaser quickly into action and if it does not do the trick put the rod down somewhere safe and pull the line with your hands. Very often this is enough to break the fine line holding the lead, which is usually the thing which gets trapped. The other point is to turn away from the direction of the bait as you pull. To alter a saying, it adds injury to insult if the lead suddenly comes free and catapults out of the water to hit you in the face.

I am a great believer in making things as easy as possible for myself when fishing. For example, it can be a considerable nuisance to carry around a large tin to hold the worms. It is much more convenient to have them in a drawstring bag with the string twisted a couple of times around a button to ensure it does not drop off. This way you have two hands free for baiting up and do not run the very real risk of dropping the tin in the river. Always add some moss to the worms a few hours before use.

There will certainly be times when you will be wading to do worming and I have already mentioned that wading can be very dangerous in parts of the Wye. Another useful tip is to have a gaff with a long strong handle which will double as a wading staff. With this over your shoulder on a sling it is immediately available to give support without removing the strap from your shoulder and is accessible when needed to gaff a fish. The rest of the essential kit, hooks, leads, fine monofilament and a small pair of scissors will all fit into the pockets and no shoulder bag is needed. There is, therefore, nothing to interfere with the use of the gaff for either of the purposes just mentioned.

Sometimes fish which have been pricked by other anglers' flies or baits are very touchy indeed and they will leap or roll over on the surface as the worms come towards them. Exciting though this may be it does not augur well for the success of your efforts and it is usually best to rest such fish for a while and try them towards evening when they are likely to be a little more cooperative.

Probably the most deadly time for worm fishing on the Wye is when the first tinge of colour comes into the water and there is just the hint of a rise on the level. This can be a very short period because salmon sense the arrival of fresh water and become anxious to move on. But if you can get amongst them before they start moving you could get some exciting fishing.

I think I should make it clear that worming is not the infallible method it is sometimes claimed to be and you have to know what you are doing to catch anything at all on it, apart from occasional flukes. However, it is admirably suited to many parts of the upper Wye and certain areas elsewhere, and its use has saved me from many unsuccessful days.

7
Salmon: Fly Fishing

Despite the improvements in spinning tackle and techniques fly fishing is still in a very healthy condition and there are many occasions when a well-presented fly will outfish any bait. From Glasbury upstream fly fishing becomes of increasing importance because the normal conditions in many of the upper parts of the river are tailor-made for the fly and cry out for its use.

In this part of the river it becomes faster, smaller and more rocky and there are numerous places where the fly can be absolutely deadly. It is also a very exciting method because, unless the fly is being fished deep early in the year, some indication of the taking fish will be seen. In addition, playing a salmon on a fly rod gives a completely different feeling from playing one on a shorter spinning rod.

Notwithstanding the fact that the upper river has by far the largest proportion of true fly water there are many places right down the river where fly can be used very successfully. Fish are often caught on the fly in the streams below Bigsweir Bridge, not far from Tintern, for example.

The Wye is a big river and Wye salmon run large so the most usual rod for fly fishing would be about 13ft 6in. Split cane is now being gradually replaced by carbon fibre which is light and very strong but there are occasional unexplained fractures with the new material which seem to indicate that it is not yet perfect. Split cane survived when hollow glass appeared and it will be interesting to see how it fares over the years against carbon fibre.

The reel must carry the line and preferably 100yd of strong backing, about 20lb breaking strain. If a new kit is being bought it is obviously better to match the reel to the rod. At a push, any large strong fly reel will do provided it has a good check but fishing is more comfortable if the weight of the reel and its contents are matched to the rod. A double-tapered sinking line will be needed at the start of the season.

In the early part of the year a 3yd length of 16lb monofilament is quite adequate as a cast. As to flies, well, in my opinion, the size is the most important factor, then the heaviness or sparseness of the dressing, followed by the lightness or darkness of the dressing. Each of these factors needs to be taken into account in deciding which fly to use and the most important consideration is the temperature of the water.

With a temperature of less than 40°F (4°C), flies of some 2 to 3in will be needed and these have to be fished as slowly as possible and right down on the stones. This is not a successful method on the Wye and very few fish are caught by its use. It may be that this is because it is difficult to get the fly down deep enough in the heavy water conditions which often prevail at the start of the season. I know that some people will insist that there is no reason why a large well-sunk fly should not catch salmon on the Wye at the start of the season but something does seem to make the method ineffective. It is true that odd fish are caught but not enough to make the fly a credible alternative to spinning. After all with the wealth of talent and experience of visiting and resident fishermen on the Wye it is unlikely that a potentially effective method would not be widely used if it could be proved to work. Whatever the reasons, when fish are about early in the season, you have to spin if you want to be seriously in the running to catch them.

As the water begins to warm up, or rather, gets less cold, fish become more active and willing to move off the bottom or to either side to take a fly and it is now, with a water temperature of something like 42–48°F(6–9°C) that normal sunk-fly fishing really comes into its own. Flies are getting smaller, 1½in to a maximum of 2in and choice of fly ranges from, for example, a heavy-winged Durham Ranger through Jock Scott to Thunder and Lightning, a Wye favourite, or Silver Wilkinson. These are all magic names and the dressings have proved over the years to be effective attractors of salmon but they are by no means a necessity and some of the exotic feathers previously thought essential to a fly, like the jungle cock, are now unobtainable. I repeat, the essentials for the choice of a suitable killing fly are the three I have already mentioned. My own favourite is a shrimp fly or Usk Grub and I am happy to use these in different sizes for most of the season when I am using a sunk fly.

There is no doubt that it is important to use a fly in which you have confidence and preferably on which you have already caught a fish. The next best thing is to use a pattern which has recently been successful for someone else on your own or adjoining water. You have to be very experienced or strong-minded to persevere and concentrate for a long time if you are fishing a strange fly which is being completely ignored. Things could so easily be exactly the same if you were fishing the 1½in Jock Scott which took that 20-pounder here yesterday, but you're not sure. When you get caught up in this sort of thing your concentration and determination slip and you catch less fish.

Choice of fly is one of those things which comes almost automatically with a little experience but there is one other very difficult factor to assess when deciding which fly to use and that is the way it is going to be fished. One man will fish a lighter pattern more slowly than another and, depending on conditions, one of them will almost certainly catch more fish than the other. To help you relinquish any permanent attachment you might have to classic fly patterns just remember that on the Wye today a great many fish are caught on tube flies in various weird and wonderful dressings as well as reasonable copies of the old pattern flies.

Again, of more importance than a precise pattern is the need to match the fly in use to the strength of the stream and height and colour of the water. In fast water a somewhat larger fly may be required to alert the fish as quickly as possible and give it that little extra time to see and take it. If the water is coloured any contrast of really dark and light dressing can be good. Also the old idea of using a bright fly on a bright day has enough truth in it to make it worth considering.

Obviously, if all these points had to be decided perfectly before fishing, no salmon flies would ever get into the water and each outing would become a torment of uncertainties. Observe the basic points and do the fine tuning as you gain experience or receive advice from more experienced fishermen. One of the nice things about fishing is that fellow anglers are nearly always generous with their knowledge.

There are many fine long streams on the Wye which are ideal fly water and many of them are easy to fish. In normal conditions the banks are often quite a lot wider than the river itself with comfortable wading from an exposed gravel edge. This is the perfect sort of place for March-to-May fishing when most salmon are likely to be found in the moderate current parts of the stream. This does not always follow and it never hurts to begin fishing a little higher than you feel necessary in order to establish a good rhythm and length of cast for when you get down to the more likely water. You never know, you might pick up a fish on the way.

Also, if you have only previously fished for trout or not fished any sort of fly before, these are the ideal places for getting used to casting with a salmon fly rod. Very briefly, cast at an angle of about 45° downstream and let the fly come around in the current until it is hanging below you. Once you have got out a good length of line which the rod will carry comfortably and you can cast smoothly, stick to it as much as possible and don't go for distance just for the sake of it.

It will probably be found that with the length of fairly heavy line that is in the water it cannot be cleanly lifted for the next cast so some line has to be drawn in. One good way to get around this is to draw in a foot or so of line when the fly drops into the water then leave things alone until the fly is below you. Then drop the rod point, slightly to one side, and pull in slowly a few more feet. Now very slowly raise the rod point until the line is beginning to move towards you, then accelerate into the back cast. The amount of line which has to be drawn in will depend on how much you are able to lift comfortably off the water with the rod. You soon get to know and it varies from person to person even with the same rod.

This is a good method for keeping everything nice and taut as far as casting is concerned and it helps to avoid the messes which can happen when you try to lift out of the water a line which has coils or bellies in it. In these cases much of the energy of the lift goes into straightening the line and instead of going cleanly back it will fall in a heap around your head. Indifferent casting can be greatly improved once this point has been grasped and a good way to really understand it is to let the line swing around into slack water at the side where it promptly goes to the bottom. Now try and lift it off and it is quite obvious that you have to shorten line and get it moving gently towards you before it will come unstuck. In a good stream even a sinking line will be held up by the current so the lift-off problem is not so acute but the principle is the same.

The elements of casting are one thing but catching salmon is another and I should say quickly that fishing with a taut line is not the way to go about seriously catching salmon, especially spring fish. In the early part of the year you are likely to be fishing water which seems almost completely devoid of fish. Certainly on the Wye they do not show much until March or April and even then the rise is a muted affair which can so easily be completely missed.

Keep a careful look-out for the head and tail rise which is a frequent indicator of a salmon ready to take a fly or bait. In a stream you may only get the briefest glimpse of a dorsal fin as the fish humps in the water but if you see it mark it down carefully and get the fly into the area as soon as you conveniently can. For most of the time you will be carefully covering water which is known to hold fish at that time of the year, without seeing anything.

Generally, cast down and across and keep the rod point at an angle to the line. When a fish does take, it is likely that you will see nothing but you could still hook it properly. The fly will be well down in the water and the line will stop or move away firmly in a manner which could not be caused by the current. When this happens or you feel a fish, tighten firmly and lean back into the rod rather than give the sudden slashing strike which can be dangerous to the cast. If the line begins to move the salmon has almost certainly got the fly in its mouth so a savage reaction is counter-productive.

Remember too that as the water begins to warm up fish will follow a fly quite a long distance so don't be in too much of a hurry to lift off the line at the end of the cast. If fish do follow your fly but do not take hold it could be that the fly is too large, so consider changing to a smaller pattern.

If the fish takes the fly as it is coming around in the current the hooking will probably be firm without much assistance from the fisherman. But if the fly is directly below when a fish takes, this is the worst position for good hooking and it is advisable to always try and tighten horizontally across the water in an effort to pull the hook into the side of the mouth. Any slight movement in the path of the fly is useful and to simply pull it straight back upstream when tightening is to risk directing the hook to the front of the mouth where there is the least area for it to obtain a secure hold.

The way one fishes these streams depends on how many other anglers there are fishing the same place. Rods are generally strictly limited except on some club or association waters. If there is plenty of time and space the best way on a wide stream is to fish it down once using a comfortable length of line, then go back to the head of the stream and start again. This time wade out a little further and cover the remaining part of the stream. This is only commonsense but frequently not done. There are just as many salmon likely to be lying on the near side or the middle of the stream as on the far side. If you wade right in at once and cast as far as you can some of the fish may see your feet and your line, but they will certainly not see the fly because it has gone well beyond them.

I remember a perfect example of this not far from Goodrich. I had always crossed a couple of fields to fish this particular stream from a gravel spit which deepened off at the edge of the stream. The accepted method was to get out well above it to begin casting and work slowly past it by edging out quietly into shallower water as the gravel bed rose again. The usual approach was not possible for some time so I had to approach the fishing from the other bank. From that side the water under the bank from which I usually fished looked completely different and where I normally waded in looked fine salmon water. The proof came when, a few casts later, my fly dropped near where the water deepened off the gravel and was promptly taken by a fine 22lb fish. No one would believe me for some time until a visiting angler did more or less the same thing. I wonder how much 'unproductive' water holds salmon but is not fished correctly.

There is no doubt whatever that there are many lies which fish better from one particular side of the river and this can only be because the fly or bait is presented to the fish in a more acceptable manner from one side than from the other. It is also true that one should not hurry through lies which are known to be good taking places. Even when fly fishing is in general use the temperature of the water may vary quite a bit from day to day and if the water happens to be on the cold side the fly will have to come quite close to the fish before it will take it.

As the general water temperature begins to move up with the advancing season fishing methods change. Casting is now done in a more square manner and as the current takes hold of the line the fly will work more quickly. When fishing across a stream it is the middle of the stream which often moves the fastest and if the line is not mended a belly of line will develop and the fly may be dragged to the surface and made to skate across the current. To take the belly out of the line or to help prevent one, do the mend as soon as the fly enters the water. Push forward with the rod and at the same time do a semi-circular clockwise flick of the point to twitch the line upstream and temporarily remove the risk of drag. In a really fast stream it may be necessary to mend the line more than once, but remember to push forward as the line is twitched or rolled otherwise the movement will be transmitted to the fly which will give a lurch in its passage through the water. In fact this is more important when using the greased-line method but it should always be taken into consideration.

In all fly fishing keep a careful watch for two potential dangers. One is the ease with which it is possible to flick a stone or the bank behind and break off the point of the hook. It is an awful waste of time to keep on fishing with a fly which proves to be useless from a hooking point of view when a salmon takes so keep a careful look out for trouble. The other thing to beware of is wind knots in the cast. On a windy day these can occur and they form more easily if the backward and forward casts are in the same plane. When possible slightly separate the planes of both casts which will go a long way towards eliminating this trouble.

From now on keep a close watch on the area of water where the fly is fishing but also keep a general watch on the water within your vision. In March and April salmon will begin to show more frequently and you are much more likely to see when a fish is taking an interest in the fly as it will be fishing nearer the surface. The thing to watch for is not a leap, which most people spot, but a quiet head and tail rise or the merest flick of a tail as a fish turns over. On the Wye at this time of year this is almost a request from the fish to be caught because it is nearly always the work of a salmon prepared to take a properly presented fly.

The inexperienced eye may miss the movement in the fairly fast-flowing busy water but once you have spotted the movement and identified it you will see rises in places where previously nothing could be seen. When you spot such a fish give him a few seconds to return to his lie then get above him and cast again so that the fly swings around over him. Move very gently back upstream a few paces if necessary to get in the right position for casting and work down to where you saw the rise rather than drop the fly right on the spot. That does not often work. If nothing happens persevere and make a few more casts and move only very slowly. If the fish still shows in the same place put on a smaller fly and go back up to your starting place again. Fortunately a fly does not normally alarm a salmon and although it may not take your fly for some reason it could quite easily do so a little later on.

Because fish get more active as the season moves on you may now see a heavy boil in the water as a salmon turns near your fly. This is the time for a cool nerve and restraint because you should not strike until the line moves away or, occasionally, stops. When it has secured the fly the fish will turn down with it and that is the time to set the hook. If you try to do so before you may well pull the fly away from the fish.

This is also the time of year when salmon are becoming more widely distributed in good numbers over a wider area of the river. It is quite impossible to be precise about this because water conditions can have such an enormous effect. The classic pattern is that a few fish are in the river at the start of the season while the upper reaches have very few. As more salmon come into the river and the season advances they spread themselves throughout the river and the upper beats start fishing well. This sort of pattern can change completely if the start of the season is really wet. When this happens, the fish in the river at the start of the season carry on running and rods at Hereford or even Hay and

A 35½lb salmon, taken by the author from the lower river

Glasbury will take a few fish. At such times the lower beats are completely out of order and the fishermen have little hope of sport.

We have also reached the time of year when it really does pay to approach the water with caution. Much of the bank length of the Wye is open and a fisherman stands out prominently on the skyline if he walks up and down to see how his favourite spot is looking. During the summer months salmon do get very shy and if you treat them with the same caution as you would trout you will not go far wrong.

There will no doubt be some rises in water level as the season progresses and the fortunes of fishermen will vary according to where they hope to fish. All parts of the river will welcome fresh water but it runs off more quickly and the beats become fishable sooner in the upper river. These places also get too low sooner than the lower beats. Even after a small flood fishing may be quite unproductive immediately below the mouth of the Ithon, depending on where the rain has fallen. If it does come in grey the Ithon makes things very difficult for fishing while above the confluence sport may be good. The Llynfi is another offender, but a red one, and the Lugg, below Hereford, can also come in thick and red.

Round about June the Wye fisherman is looking forward to the hoped-for run of grilse. If they come in good numbers they can provide excellent fishing at a time when the stock of other salmon may be sadly depleted. Grilse fishing is rather like a midway method between conventional sunk-fly salmon fishing and wet-fly fishing for trout. Grilse are often caught by anglers using the 13ft 6in rod and sunk fly but the chances of success are higher and the sport better if the scale of the equipment is reduced when grilse are about. A 10ft, fairly heavy, trout rod is ideal with double taper line and as much backing as the reel will hold, but not less than 50yd. You never know what might take the fly. A tapered cast of 2yd or a little more is long enough for most situations because grilse are not tackle-shy. The flies are small and lightly dressed, not more than 1in in length.

Now we move into the rougher shallow water for some of our sport, and it is surprising how shallow the water can be and still hold grilse. As with all sorts of fly fishing it pays to be prepared to change flies and tactics to cover varying conditions. Where the water is really rough a cast with a 10–12lb point can be used but where the water is more streamy 10lb would be sufficient. This must, of course, be decided by taking into account how easy or difficult it will be to play a fish in the spot you are fishing.

With the water temperature now upwards of 50°F(10°C) it is

quite in order, and in fact necessary, for the fly to move more quickly and be near the surface of the water. The fly is fished rather more square than in the early part of the year and it will be necessary to keep a watch for drag which becomes much more obvious when the fly is fishing near the surface.

Long casting may not be necessary but because the fish are likely to be widely spread over shallow water great care is needed in approaching them. Throughout the summer salmon fishing should be treated, in this respect, just like trout fishing and all experienced trout fishermen are aware of the absolute necessity for keeping out of sight of the fish as much as possible and moving quietly and cautiously. Cover the close-in water before extending the length of the casts and drop the fly as gently as possible. When the cast has been fished out twitch the line a little before recasting. Grilse are quick takers and, unlike their bigger early-season relatives, have to be tightened on as soon as a take is felt or the line seen to move. These little fish can be killed quite quickly on the light tackle as long as conditions are reasonable. Fortunately, grilse often fight near the surface jumping frequently and expending their energy. This is not surprising when it is remembered that they are frequently found in shallow water.

Morning and evening are the best times for grilse fishing with particular attention being given to the evenings. Before the sun gets too high and as it is setting are both good times for finding the grilse in a cooperative mood. The majority of us have to make the most of the available time so we tend to carry on fishing during the heat of the day. When fishing in this manner and a salmon shows an interest in the fly but does not take hold, let him see it again. Then, if the same thing happens, change the fly for a smaller one.

The method I have described for grilse fishing is only one step removed from greased-line fishing and it is a natural step too. Mastery of greased-line fishing will certainly increase the odds in our favour when fishing conditions get really difficult in the summer but, let's make no mistake about it, greased-line fishing is not a magic formula which is always going to catch a salmon when everything else fails.

The grilse kit mentioned above will be fine for greased-line work, but now we use a floating line and there is no need for grease, except occasionally on part of the cast to ensure that the fly is kept only just below the surface of the water. The idea is to cast square across or even slightly upstream and let the fly swim broadside on to the current with no drag. We want the fly to float naturally and limply, just as though it were quite unattached to anything.

Flies can be smaller than the ones used for grilse fishing and they can be very lightly dressed indeed. It is amazing just how much a salmon can see even in rough water, because it is the surface only which is really disturbed. Conditions on the Wye are not really clear enough, in my opinion, for the use of almost bare hooks and I do not consider these extremes of technique necessary or wise.

In addition, most fishermen would have little confidence in fishing an almost bare hook and that is going to limit their chances of success straight away. We do not have enormous hatches of flies on the Wye and I cannot recall any occasion when I have seen salmon busily sucking in hatching flies in quantity. Nevertheless, a small fly fished just under the surface can be very good and it will undoubtedly take salmon when other methods completely fail.

The main problem is stopping the fly from skating across the surface of the water and it needs constant vigilance to avoid this happening. Sometimes the centre of the stream will be the fastest while on other occasions it will be the nearest or farthest water which causes the trouble. Practice mending the line until you can get it done easily and with a minimum of disturbance to the fly. If it is the farther water which is fastest then a long mend has to be done and this is the most difficult to do without twitching the fly. Not that this is all that important unless a fish is coming at the fly at the instant it is pulled. If the stream is particularly awkward a couple of mends may have to be made during the course of the cast.

It often pays to keep the rod fairly high when fishing the greased-line method. The very clever idea behind the method is that slack line is given when a fish takes the fly. The line bellies downstream of the fish and a sideways tightening sets the hook in the scissors of the jaw. It is said, quite rightly, that far more salmon are lost through striking too soon than from striking too late but this does not always hold good if there are numbers of grilse about. Try the accepted method first—giving slack then tightening sideways—but, if the fish is missed, try the fish again and tighten more quickly when the rise comes. Unless the fish is pricked it will very probably rise at the fly again.

On bright days there are frequently short periods when clouds move across the sun and obscure it and these can be deadly moments, whichever fly-fishing method is in use. Fish which have splashed at a fly or turned away at the last moment become much bolder when the sun is hidden so keep a watch for the approach of these moments. If clouds are about mark down a moving fish and try him as they obscure the sun.

If your fly should happen to be taken by one of the larger spring or summer fish a lively time will ensue if it decides to go out of the pool and you cannot stop it. On the upper river particularly there are numerous areas of uneven and slippery rocks and you need the balance of a mountain goat to get after the quarry quickly and remain in one piece!

August is usually a really bad month for all kinds of salmon fishing on the Wye. If the weather is considered good for most other purposes it will be grim for the salmon fisherman. Bare rocks and shrunken pools in the upper reaches and heavy weed growth in many places further down coincide with a time when most available fish have seen everything the angler has to offer and are no longer interested. Also, low water deters fresh fish from coming in from the estuary. They stay out there waiting for the signal that fresh water is coming.

At such times even fly fishing amounts to flogging a dead horse but the small almost floating fly does at least give a reasonable chance of finding a fish ready to make a fatal mistake. It may still require a lot of hard fishing to make it happen.

Very occasionally a fish will be picked up in the heat of the day using light trout tackle with a floating line and a small trout wet fly. A 2yd cast is long enough and you may have to grease part of the cast to keep the fly just under the surface. This again is hard work for the results which are likely to be achieved but it must be admitted that it is quite a triumph to land a salmon when everyone else has given up trying. It helps to vary the monotony and you could always pick up a few good trout.

When the evening arrives and the sun goes down and the air begins to cool the time has come to start thinking about serious fishing. Now is the time to get out the big spring fishing kit with a 2yd cast of 16lb monofilament. My favourite fly for this game is a big 2in terror, a large tube fly sometimes wound around with a little fine lead wire to give the terror extra weight. A suitable needle-sharp treble completes the outfit.

Make sure that everything needed is to hand and properly assembled because you will be fishing the last hour of light and will have no time to take off the cast and retie everything if you start to fish only to find that the line is around the rod. Stick to one or two likely spots as close together as possible because, again, time spent walking from one place to another is valuable fishing time lost. At this time in the evening fish are frequently found in the shallow quick water where the tail of one pool picks up to drop into the stream of the next. This is typical upper-river water. If you keep a look-out during the evening you will often see a fish or two roll over in these places so try to mark their positions by reference to a rock or tree or other landmark. Don't go near the pools for an hour or more before the 'evening shift'.

When the time comes, with not more than an hour before dark (not dusk), move quietly along the bank or into the water and begin casting down and across. Keep the rod point high as the fly swings around. It is surprising how much you can see on the water even quite late in the evening. Anyway, at this time of year it seldom gets really dark at night and there is usually a hint of light. The line will show up quite clearly if the water is fairly smooth and the terror may skate across the surface, especially when the rod is held up. During the daytime this would be very likely to put fish off but not in the evening or at least, not always. Sometimes they prefer the terror just under the surface but they are often attracted by the wake as it swings on the surface. When using this method the take is a strong one. It is very exciting to see a great swirl in the water and then feel the heavy drag of a fish as it takes. On no account should you strike until you actually feel the fish. If the light is right you see everything virtually in sharp black and white and you have to be well disciplined not to strike at the rise. You will nearly always pull the fly from the fish or just prick it if you strike too soon.

You should be able to control the fight fairly easily with the heavy tackle and it is just as well if, as so often happens, you hook a fish just as the light is getting so bad that you know you will very soon have to stop fishing. It is helpful, late in the evening, to have a companion available to gaff the fish or net it for you because in the excitement of playing the fish in gathering gloom you may unwittingly forget to feel your way carefully, and lifting the feet instead of sliding them could result in a nasty fall. In spite of the obvious disadvantages of late evening fishing I think this must be about the most exciting way of catching salmon. There are lots of places ideally suited to this method on the Wye.

As with bait fishing, things improve as autumn approaches. Water levels move up and temperatures slip down and salmon will take a fly more freely than they would in the heat of summer. The need for tiny sparsely-dressed flies is over and unless the year is a freak one and water levels remain low and clear, 1–1½in flies can be used. These are usually fished with a sinking line but higher in the water and somewhat faster than in spring. Remember that a gaff may not be used from 1 September so fish will have to be netted, tailed or beached.

8
Trout

Each year large trout are taken from the Wye and its tributaries and some really good fish are caught. A specimen of 5lb 13oz was caught on the Irfon in 1977, a 3½lb fish at Holme Lacy, numerous fish over 2lb on the Monnow and a 3-pounder from the confluence of the Lugg and Wye. A 2lb trout is not all that uncommon in many of the upper waters such as Glasbury, Builth and Rhayader and in tributaries like the Ithon, Irfon, upper Lugg and Arrow. But taking into account the size of the Wye system and the large area of apparently good trout water the river cannot be called a major one as far as the trout fisherman is concerned.

Numbers of trout are tending to fall and quite a lot of stocking is done, both in the upper waters of the Wye itself and in the tributaries, to try and maintain stocks and provide good fishing. It is surprising that the river does not at present have the ability to take care of the replacement of fish caught on its own. Several theories have been advanced, such as the lack of suitable food, but when we think of the enormous number of salmon fry that the Wye supports and the ever-spreading and increasing numbers of coarse fish this is a far from convincing idea and much too simple.

My own view is that there are several simple contributing factors which, added together, have produced a complex problem that is going to be very hard to solve. First there are places, such as the top of the Tarenig and the Irfon, where food is very scarce due partly to problems with the old lead workings. In addition there is now an enormously increased demand for fishing, both from coarse fishermen and game fishermen. The problem here is not only one of straight-forward demand because the situation is complicated by the methods of fishing. A trout fisherman will try to take as many trout as he can, or is allowed.

The coarse fisherman returns virtually all the fish he catches with, dare I say it, the exception of the trout. This, added to the fact that coarse fish, generally, are more vigorous in the survival stakes, puts the trout at a great disadvantage. There is a good case to be made for the removal or killing, if they cannot be placed elsewhere, of a lot of coarse fish and this should benefit the quality of the coarse fishing as well as the trout fishing.

Less trout means less breeding stock and more pressure on those that remain and the trout could, eventually, get squeezed out of existence. The water authority does some electric fishing in an effort to reduce the numbers of coarse fish in predominantly trout waters. There have been instances where these fish have been offered to owners in other waters who have refused to take them unless the authority delivered them as well, free of charge. The accepted trout waters still retain a good head of trout, but the coarse fish stocks must be carefully monitored in the future if this balance is to be maintained.

Trout fishing on the Wye starts on 1 March and the season finishes on 30 September. By the beginning of March many trout, particularly in the main river, are back in quite decent condition. This varies from year to year according to how severe the winter has been. After a really hard winter with snow-water still in the brooks keeping down the temperature of the main river, trout will not regain anything like decent condition for several weeks after the opening of the fishing season. The upper Wye and upper tributaries also tend to be a little late in producing good fish because of the low temperature of the water. Tributaries like the Monnow, which is mostly slow flowing, rarely have such problems and will produce fine fish right from the start of the season. In fact, the Monnow is probably the best trout fishery on the whole of the Wye system.

The ideal method for catching trout is fly fishing and both dry fly and wet fly are widely used. You can, of course, do all your fly fishing for trout on the Wye with just one crisp-actioned rod of about 8ft 6in and manage quite well. But if you fish any of the more overgrown tributaries and also use wet fly, three rods are better and help to eliminate some of the difficulties and problems which can arise when a single compromise rod is used.

The 8ft 6in rod will deal excellently with all dry-fly work on the main river and most of the tributaries but if you get around with your fishing you will inevitably come across places which are badly overgrown, and in these places a shorter rod, down to 7ft 6in, can be a great help. It's amazing how much easier it is to fish these difficult places with a rod which is just one foot shorter than usual. I should keep this rod in reserve and only use it when absolutely necessary, when it will be very helpful. Until the trees and bankside growth get really bad it is much better to persevere with the longer rod.

The smaller waters hold trout which, by the nature of their surroundings, are shy and easily scared. If conditions force you to fish right on top of them you have to be extremely cautious in your movements to achieve any consistent success.

For wet-fly fishing I prefer an easier-action rod and for the Wye my ideal length would be 9ft to 9ft 6in. It is interesting how ideas and fashions change with the times. This is inevitable I suppose but I am not convinced that the changes are all pure gain. Modern rods are light and strong and getting shorter, but putting into words my ideas about the rods I now use reminds me of how we used to fish. Fifteen or more years ago a favourite rod for wet-fly fishing was a 13ft 6in light greenheart. These rods had slow, leisurely actions and were rested partly on the inside of the thigh. They could be seen in many places on rivers like the Wye and Usk and once you got used to them they almost did the fishing for you. This type of rod covered large amounts of water with a minimum of effort and the hook was set by a gentle lift of the rod. Returning to the present day, material for any of the rods mentioned for today's use can be split cane, hollow glass or carbon fibre. Carbon fibre is essentially light and very strong but there have been reports of unexplained fractures with these rods so there are still occasional problems.

Whichever type of rod you use do make sure that the line is the right weight for it because this makes for much more comfortable fishing. The Association of Fishing Tackle Makers (AFTM) number is stamped on most fly rods and is a useful guide but remember that the number is based on the weight of the first ten yards of line, excluding the first yard. If you are likely to be doing very short casting a somewhat heavier line should be bought. If you will frequently be looking for distance, it might pay to buy a slightly lighter line.

I have no doubt that on the Wye and its tributaries the best all-round line is a double taper. It requires a little more effort to get out enough double-taper line to really begin working the rod than is necessary with a forward taper but the advantage shows the moment the fly is deposited on the water. In most hands the double taper drops the fly, and itself, much more gently on the surface and there is altogether less disturbance. This is quite an advantage on the Wye where you are likely to be fishing water which is low and clear and sometimes hard-fished as well.

A good breaking strain for the point of the cast is 2lb unless you are going to fish a place where big trout are more likely to be found or there are lots of snags. In these cases a point of 3 to 4lb may be necessary, the final decision depending on how delicate your touch is. A 2yd cast is quite long enough for all dry-fly work on the Wye. This length is much easier to control than the 3yd cast and in breezy weather the fly can be presented more accurately to the fish.

I make all my own casts and strongly recommend the practice. You simply need three reels of monofilament, heavy, medium and light, a matchstick to help pull the monofilament through the loops and a few minutes' time.

Forming the knots is very easy. To join together two lengths, overlap them, make a loop and pull through one pair of ends twice. Ease the knot together. For the final tightening I often moisten the knot in my mouth before firming it up. Don't pull too tightly; it isn't necessary and in the lower breaking strains overtightening may bruise and weaken the monofilament. To form the loop of the cast, bend over about 4in of the heavy monofilament, make a loop with it around the double thickness and pass twice through the loop before tightening. These simple knots will not slip unless you try to join very heavy line to very fine line, which you should never do anyway. Incidentally, the waste can be cut off really tight to the knot unless you are making a wet-fly cast. In this case the lower end of the waste can be left to form droppers.

You can, if you wish, use more than three thicknesses of monofilament to obtain a more even taper but, whichever way you do it, use slightly shorter lengths of each size as you come

The author fly fishing on the Upper Wye

down the cast. When making your own casts in the manner I have described you can vary the length and weights to suit the conditions and this should frequently make fishing easier and more comfortable.

Having established that the upper Wye and tributaries are the best trout water it is as well to point out that trout are caught right down the river although they are only locally distributed in small pockets where conditions happen to suit them. Anywhere where there is a break in the normal glide to give a stream over clean gravel is likely to have its modest trout population. The compensation for lack of numbers is that the fish are on average considerably bigger than they are further upstream.

The most popular dry flies for the Wye are March Brown, Olive Dun, Greenwell's Glory, Pheasant Tail and sometimes an Alder or Grannom. An interesting and popular fly is the reverse-dressed Pheasant Tail which has the hackle near the bend. The arrangement is said to aid presentation, which may or may not be true. Some mayfly are found most years, but not in very large numbers.

Exact imitation of the fly on the water is of far less importance than good presentation and this means a lot more than just dropping the fly gently. In fact it is not much use dropping them lightly and carefully if you have already sent the fish rushing in all directions in panic. This will certainly happen if you splash about carelessly and under difficult summer conditions it is amazing just how careful you have to be. To prove the point, wade ordinarily into the water of a smooth flat on a wind-free evening and see how the disturbance spreads. The ripple goes on and on and never seems to stop. Although the effect is obviously not so pronounced in rougher water the principle is the same and when wading it is always essential to move smoothly and as little as possible.

Incidentally, parts of the upper Wye, the rocky parts, and similar places in tributaries are absolute murder for wading. Ordinary rubber soles are quite useless in this sort of place and studs are only a very modest improvement. The best protection comes from thick felt pads on the soles. I can assure you that this is not a fad because it takes much of the pleasure out of fishing if you are constantly in fear of losing your footing. It can also be very dangerous if you slide into a deep part of the river and your waders fill with water. So, please, be careful and well prepared.

In the early part of the season, about March and even early April after a severe winter, trout are still regaining some condition. Food will have been scarce because of the very cold water and things can be particularly hard in the upper parts of tributaries and the brooks. At such times the main river is probably the best bet from about Builth downstream to, say, Holme Lacy. The Monnow should be good as should the upper Lugg and Arrow, all fairly slow-moving waters.

The best of the fishing for the first weeks of the season is to be had during the period of about one hour before and after midday. This is usually the warmest part of the day and the time when flies hatch out and if there is a hatch of march browns the fishing can be good. Before and after this time conditions are often too cold for much sport on the dry fly. It is amazing how quickly the sun disappears just as it was starting to make its presence felt and leaves us in no doubt that winter is only just over.

The more usual method at the start of the season is wet fly. The traditional method of wet-fly fishing is to cast down and across but, where the width of the water allows it, I find it much more effective to cast almost square across. This is because the downstream cast always puts you in the weakest position for hooking trout. The tendency is to pull the fly away from them on the strike or to hook them very lightly in the front of the mouth. Downstream bites are usually positive strong plucks because the fly or flies are working at the end of a line held taut by the current. A different technique is needed with the square cast.

As the flies drop into the water pull in just enough slack line to put you in contact with the flies without dragging them. Then follow around with the rod point as the line comes around and keep watching the spot where the line enters the water. Strike firmly but not too quickly at any unusual stoppage or hesitation of the line and you will not go far wrong. The very obvious and exciting downstream bites are more than compensated for by the much better hooking of this method, often in the side of the mouth. If the water is narrow or other circumstances force you to fish downstream try and tighten sideways when a fish takes.

Some good wet flies for the Wye are the wet versions of the dry flies previously mentioned, Greenwell's Glory, March Brown, Pale Olive, February Red and Wickham's Fancy. In recent years Mallard and Claret has become popular but my own undoubted favourite wet fly for the Wye is an Invicta. This is quite a heavily dressed fly and yet it does very well with most other fish as well as trout. The other patterns may be very lightly dressed and yet they will go on catching fish even when they have been almost shredded by fishes' teeth. As with dry flies, the usual size hook for these wet flies would be a 12.

Incidentally, if you still prefer to fish downstream it is interesting to note that some people prefer to use a stiffer hackle, more like a cock hackle, than the traditional back-swept hen hackle normally used. The idea is that the harder hackle is more lively when the fly is held on a tight line in the force of the current. The soft hackle simply wraps itself around the fly. This may or may not be so but it is an interesting viewpoint. It is in any case becoming increasingly difficult to get good quality cock hackles because birds are not kept long enough for the brightness and maturity to develop in the feathers. For my own part I like the drowned look given by the soft hackle and the few times I have experimented along the lines indicated the results were inconclusive.

It is advisable to fish the quieter streams and glides or the edges of fast water early in the season. Leave the rougher places for later in the year when the water has warmed up and fish are strong enough to cope with the heavier current and higher oxygen content.

One needs to be very careful when making positive statements about fishing. It is very easy to accept things at their face value and come to a completely wrong conclusion. A typical example is where we are using two flies when wet-fly fishing. One of the flies nearly always attracts the most fish, in fact it often happens that the one fly will take four or five fish to the other's one. The natural conclusion is that the successful fly is more attractive to the trout but this may not be the case at all. It could be that the successful fly is fishing the water at a more acceptable depth for the trout so it is taken in preference to the other. Try putting on two of the successful flies. My experience has been that it is often the same fly that goes on catching the fish.

This means that the height in the water at which the flies fish can be very important, particularly early in the year. If trout are taking near the surface it will be necessary to grease part of the cast to keep the flies well up. On other days, when the fish are feeding near the bottom you have to treat the cast to make it sink.

Although there are plenty of large open flats on the Wye I think it is safer to use no more than two flies. Three may cover the water better but there is much more risk of one of them fouling the net at a crucial moment.

If the trout are dour and offers few and far between try letting the flies hang in the current when they get directly below and the cast would normally be considered fished out. Move the rod up and down and twitch the line with the left hand. This will sometimes produce a take when all else fails. Don't forget the strike to the side or you will lose a high proportion of the fish you have persuaded to take.

As the season progresses the upper waters and tributaries become a better bet. Bankside vegetation is still at a minimum and the normally overgrown places are worth fishing now before everything starts to grow. The Lugg tributaries like the Arrow, Frome, Pinsley and Stretford brooks come under this category. There is a fair amount of silt in the Lugg itself but the Arrow has a lot of clean gravel. By May trout should be in splendid shape and in their permanent summer quarters. Tributaries like the Elan, Marteg and Edw are worthy of attention. The Elan has a lot of rock, particularly in the upper parts, but plenty of gravel in the lower reaches. The Marteg, a fairly open tributary, also has a mixture of rock and gravel and the Edw much the same. The trouting can be quite good in these tributaries and we must not forget the Ithon and Irfon. Both these tributaries flow in broad-based valleys and below Penybont the Ithon is quite slow-flowing for some distance. The Ithon runs through a lot of open country but is not as rugged as the upper Wye. There are some areas of bedrock but a lot of gravel. Around Llanwrtyd Wells, the Irfon is mostly rock-bottomed with gullies but below Llanwrtyd there is much more gravel. Both valleys are overlooked by hills. Many parts of both these tributaries get quite a hammering and a fair amount of restocking is done.

The ideal method now is dry fly and in the right hands this can be a deadly method of catching trout. As I have said before exact imitation is not very important and a Greenwell, Pheasant Tail or March Brown on a 12 hook is all that is required. In fact for my own fishing I often use a simple no-name pattern. A strand of pheasant-tail feather forms the body with yellow tying silk, the Whisks are pheasant tail and the hackle a bright glassy ginger cock. My supply of these hackles is running out and I doubt whether I shall be able to replace them when the fatal day arrives. The great thing about these hackles is that they float like little tugboats, without having to use too many turns, and they are very easy to see in the popply water.

In many places on the Wye good rises are not all that frequent and you have to fish the water rather than the rise. In the daytime cover the rough streams and runs carefully, whenever possible fishing upstream and moving very cautiously.

If you cannot pick out the fly when it lands gauge the spot where you feel it should be and let the eye move unhurriedly down with the pace of the current. Keep a general look-out rather than fixing your eyes on one spot and don't allow yourself to be diverted by anything outside that field of vision. A rise will show as a quiet flick in the stream and if it is anywhere near where you feel the fly should be, tighten at once. Some of these rough places can be quite tricky to fish, hence my devotion to the ginger hackle. The parachute type of fly is a good floater too, particularly when, like so many commercial flies, they are tied with soft hackles. The method of tying exposes more of the hackle to the surface of the water so it floats better. Unfortunately it has a lower profile in the water because of the way it is tied. Nevertheless it is a good fly.

Almost as tricky for fishing, especially on a bright day, are the comparatively smooth stream edges and gentle runs near the bank. These often carry along bubbles of foam and small fragments of floating debris which can easily mask the fly from unskilled eyes. If these places also give you trouble in keeping track of the fly remember what I have said about the rough places. Estimate the position, relax the eyes and follow downstream at the pace of the current. This is simply a knack but it takes some anglers longer to acquire it than others.

I suppose the average trout cast is about twelve yards so exceptional eyesight is not required. Also, most fishermen cast in the same manner all the time unless conditions force a change. It is possible, therefore, to judge quite accurately how the line will extend and where the fly will be and I know fishermen with dubious eyesight who know exactly where the fly is under the most trying conditions, but it is so much easier if your eyesight is good.

Keep a bottle of fly floatant in your pocket and be meticulous about keeping that fly floating on its points. If it starts to sink or you catch a fish, dry the fly really thoroughly before trying to oil it. If the fly gets covered in slime from a fish give it a good swill in the river before attending to it. One of the most effective ways of drying a fly is to squeeze it firmly between the folds of a well-laundered linen handkerchief, not a new one. Hold the fly in the handkerchief until all the moisture has been extracted then blow briskly into the back of the fly to reform it and make the hackle stand up well. The fly is now ready for waterproofing.

Towards dusk trout tend to leave the streams and move up onto nearby shallow flats. The gentle dimples you see on the smooth surface belie the fact that they may be made by large trout. Again, where possible, try to fish upstream and into the failing light. Using the light in this manner enables you to take advantage of the reflection off the water and you can fish comfortably and successfully when many other fishermen have gone home. Do be careful when wading though. A reasonable disturbance from a fly line will probably not put the trout down but the ripple from waders almost certainly will. By the time they come back on, the light may have got too bad for further fishing. If you can possibly get the dark mass of a bank behind you, try to cover some of the fish without wading at all.

It is a good idea to carry a spare cast or two with a fly already mounted. Winding them on a card is helpful because it enables you to remove them with little risk of getting them tangled in the failing light and losing valuable fishing time.

A method which does require good eyesight is nymph fishing. We have already seen that there are many times on the Wye system when you have to fish the water rather than the rise but this should not deter you from using a nymph. The classic method of nymph fishing is to stalk the trout of the clear chalk streams and cast up to them from behind, endeavouring to arrange things so that the nymph arrives in the right place as the fish moves from side to side.

This is rarely possible on the Wye so the nymph is used in the manner of the upstream wet fly. You should be using a floating line and the best results come when the nymph fishes the water at or very near the depth at which the trout are feeding. To achieve this get some of the 2yd cast under the surface of the water by wiping it over with glycerine, but don't overdo it. The idea is to have as much of the cast on the surface as possible so that it can be seen and kept straight. Wye trout will often be taken with this method at about mid-water but the position does vary quite a lot. It is quite simple to vary the fishing position of the nymph by using liquid paraffin where necessary to float the cast and the glycerine to get part of it under the water. Be prepared to make changes in the position of the nymph if offers do not come. Besides trout, grayling, dace and chub are all frequently caught by this method so there should be some bites on most days to show that you have got the fishing level about right.

The main difficulty with nymph fishing comes in spotting and hooking the take. The pronounced pluck felt in downstream wet-fly fishing rarely occurs and the presence of a fish is usually indicated by a simple hesitation of the cast where it enters the water. Raise the rod point smartly as soon as this is seen or suspected and you should hook a fair number of takes. Once identification of the takes has been mastered the proportion of secure hookings should be high.

A March Brown pattern is very successful on the Wye but almost anything similar will do. You can use two contrasting patterns if you like and, in fact, two wet fly patterns like a Hare's Ear and a March Brown fished in the upstream manner can be almost as good. The main requirement is to keep a really close watch on the behaviour of the cast where it enters the water.

While caution is necessary when moving on the main river it

is even more important on the tributaries and their own feeders. Some of these get very small and shallow. Walk quietly up to this type of water and you may catch a glimpse of a few black shapes streaking away. The chances are that if you have got close enough to see the fish they will have seen you and acted accordingly.

Some places will be overgrown but generally the upper waters and tributaries get faster and more open. On the open waters I like to use as long a rod as I can. A light 9ft or 9ft 6in helps to put distance between the fisherman and the fish but this is a matter of choice and temperament and many anglers are quite happy with shorter rods.

Upstream fishing is best and where it can be avoided, don't wade. Kneeling and crawling are the two main requirements here and it would be hard not to overemphasise the shyness and initial caution of the fish found in these places. Anything strange will send them scurrying for cover and if this happens you can forget the spot and move on. But if you can get the fly to them without disturbing them they will take freely. In this connection it is all too easy to forget that although you may be behind the fish, if the sun is behind you, you could be throwing a huge shadow yards ahead and on to the water.

Use a fine cast with a point of not more than 2lb breaking strain for these waters. The fish are mostly small and if you occasionally hook something larger than average you should be alright if you take care. Just remember to tighten and not strike, a most unfortunate word when discussing fine fishing, whether it be for trout or coarse fish.

It is on the bushy, snaggy waters that a rather heavier cast should be used. For fishing this sort of area I should use a cast with a point of about 4lb breaking strain and only 1½yd long. Casting in the conventional sense is often impossible and switching or dapping may be needed.

Again, great caution is required, particularly at the moment the cast is made. All the good work of a careful approach can be undone if, at the last moment, you move hurriedly or stand up to get a better view. Normal upstream methods may have to be replaced by improvisation and the fly put on the water wherever possible, upstream, downstream, across or dapped.

I like to travel light, especially when fishing in tributaries. Spare flies, scissors, casts, a bottle of floatant and fly-drying material will all go in the pockets. I use a small basket for holding fish because it is light and airy and keeps the fish fresh. The net is, in my case, a compromise. For convenience a folding net is ideal but to give most help where it is not easy to get to the water I prefer a rigid, fairly long-handled, net. I would rather curse each time this gets caught up somewhere than reach for the folding net when playing a fish only to find it had been pulled out by a bush 60yd or so downstream.

Some anglers are bothered far more by flies than others and if you are one of the unfortunate ones you will know what I mean. Carry a small bottle of repellent, just in case. Flies and midges can be present in enormous numbers in the summer and they can make fishing a misery if you have no protection against them.

Watch out for salmon parr on the Wye and tributaries. These eager little fish will hurl themselves upon any fly in the neighbourhood and large numbers are hooked and killed each year. Observance of the size limit virtually puts the matter beyond doubt even if you are not sure whether it is a parr or trout you have hooked. There is no excuse for killing and keeping salmon parr. On the Wye and tributaries above Rhayader Bridge the size limit for trout is 7in from the tip of the snout to the fork of the tail. Below Rhayader Bridge a measurement of 8in must be observed.

Parr can usually be identified as soon as they are hooked by their quick darting manner but they are instantly recognisable when taken from the water. Trout normally hang still until they are touched but parr go on wriggling like mad until returned to the water. Moisten the hand before holding these small salmon for unhooking and slide them gently back into the water—don't throw them.

There are further differences between small trout and parr. The little adipose fin of the parr is grey while that of the trout has a reddish tip; the tail of the parr is decidedly more forked than that of the trout and the mouth smaller; the visible maxillary bone of the parr ends little over half-way below the centre of the eye while that of the trout ends past the eye.

Along the tributaries bushes and undergrowth seem to take on

Afan Marteg, a tributary of the Wye, pictured between Rhayader and Llangurig

lives of their own and they delight in attaching themselves to you and your gear. Slow, smooth movements eliminate most of the problems and scratches but they don't stop the fly getting caught up. When, despite your best efforts, you still get caught around a branch or in a bush the fate of the fly is usually decided immediately. If you get impatient and pull hard the hook will probably bed itself into a twig or leaf and you then have to put down the rod and pull by hand until the cast comes free or, more likely, a break occurs. It is much better to ease the line tight, very gently, and pull slowly. In many cases you will see the cast uncurling from the branch or slipping out of the bush towards you. This is another danger moment and in bad places the line should be held in the left hand close to the rod so that it can be sharply pulled at once, if necessary. There is nothing more annoying than working carefully to free a fly only to have it drop straight into another trap.

An excellent method for large or small waters on the Wye is the upstream worm. On the main river and open tributaries a light spinning rod and fixed-spool reel will be best. Use a 3lb or possibly 4lb line and load the drum fully so that line will slip easily over the lip. A good-quality hook, about size 8, and a worm of about 3in should be about right. As already mentioned, worms are much tougher and more lively if kept for a few hours in thick moss before use. If you use a long shank hook you can run the worm around the bend of the hook and a little up the shank. I prefer simply to pass the hook through the worm slightly nearer the head than tail. I believe this leaves the worm freer and more active and it certainly lasts longer.

The idea is to cast the worm as gently as possible and drop it upstream in runs, streams and likely eddies. To keep the presentation as natural as possible use a minimum of lead. The shot should be really soft so that they can be removed and changed easily without damaging the fine line. Begin with one shot, about a BB, some six inches from the worm which will help to give accuracy to the casting but leave the worm fairly free to move about in the water.

As the bait comes back towards you it should touch the bottom fairly often but only lightly. Reel in carefully to keep in close touch with the bait and when the line stops, be careful. It could simply be that the lead has snagged a pebble in which case a slight lift of the rod should free it. But if this happens too frequently you have too much lead on and a shot should be removed. The method is quite a sensitive one and you should be prepared to vary the number and weight of shot frequently when water conditions change.

When a trout is interested in the worm the line will tremble, stop or move sideways. When any one of these movements occurs you need to slack off line, either by opening the bale arm or moving forward a step. After a few seconds tighten and the trout should be hooked. The time required before striking can vary considerably and depends on how hungry the fish are and what the water conditions are like. When the fish are going well, two or three seconds will be sufficient but if they are not taking well and are rather edgy anything up to ten seconds may be needed. You need to get the timing right otherwise you will either miss fish or hook them in the throat. If the latter happens, small fish or salmon parr may be killed and no real angler wants this to happen. Apart from anything else the killing of salmon parr and undersized trout is, of course, illegal. Early morning in the summer with low clear water conditions is the best time to adopt this method and if there is a light breeze to ruffle the water, so much the better.

On bushy, overgrown waters the worm is more versatile than the fly and it can be manoeuvered into places that no fly could get anywhere near. Strangely enough a fly rod is probably the ideal implement for worm fishing in these places. You can use the ordinary double-taper fly line but a light level line is better. The cast need be only 1½yd or even 1yd in really tight places.

A very useful side cast can be made by holding the bait in the left hand and pulling back to flex the rod, which is then flicked horizontally. You cannot hope to reach as far with this kit as with the spinning outfit but for difficult places it is delightfully precise in dropping the bait just where it is wanted.

Spinning is another method widely used on the Wye for trout and it accounts for a lot of fish, particularly the big ones. Spinning is not really suited to the small upper waters and indeed can be very difficult, if not impossible, to use there. If you enjoy spinning concentrate on the main river below Rhayader. As you come downstream trout get fewer but they certainly get bigger and there are fine fish to be caught. These old stagers are cannibals in the true sense and they like nothing better than a meal of small trout or salmon parr. Their capture is a good thing for the river. The big trout are not quite so fussy about having clean gravel on the river bottom as the smaller fish, probably because of their feeding habits.

The summer trout spinner has to face the same conditions of low clear water so beloved by the upstream wormer but the conditions are not so well suited to spinning. Virtually the same tackle can be used—light spinning rod and fixed-spool reel with a line of 3–4lb breaking strain. Popular baits are small Mepps, quill minnows and devons of not more than 1in. My own favourite colour minnow is gold but a blue and silver is the firm choice of other fishermen. For most baits except the quill minnow you need only add a swivel, about 18in from the bait, and a small anti-kink vane immediately above it. In the case of a quill minnow or other really light bait you can dispense with the anti-kink vane and substitute a tiny jardine lead bent into an anti-kink shape after twisting it onto the line above the swivel. Keep extraneous bits on the line to a minimum to cut down disturbance of the water.

Trout will take a spun bait in the glare of midday if they are really hungry but early morning is usually the best time. If fish are in an uncertain mood you may see them flash as they turn away or spot a dark shape following close behind the bait. When this happens try casting from a different angle and winding a little more quickly. When trout are in this difficult mood I much prefer a tiny Mepps to any of the conventional minnows.

If you happen to start fishing just as the water begins to rise from rain in the hills sport can be really good. In the upper reaches the level can start to rise quite rapidly and it then drops just as quickly once the rain has passed. The colour normally goes quickly too because the upper Wye generally runs clear however high it may be. The grey outpouring of the Ithon can, of course, alter that. When the water is fairly high and coloured, fish down and across to give the fish more time to see the bait.

Spinning with a natural minnow is undoubtedly one of the best ways of catching the big Wye trout. Mounted on a small spinning flight the natural bait often proves more deadly than any artificial sort but there is the bother of obtaining and mounting the minnows. In addition they can be easily damaged and are fair game to other predatory fish. Having said all that the devotees of natural minnow spinning feel that the results more than outweigh the disadvantages and they are quite happy to take the time and trouble needed to enable them to use the method.

I must admit that my own best Wye trout, a brownie of just 4lb fell to a large lobworm being freelined under a bankside bush in about three feet of water late on a summer evening. I knew he was there and I was not alone. The fish had been bombarded with fly and spinner for several days before it took the lob.

There is a small population of rainbow trout in the Wye, very locally distributed. They have been caught in the Monnow, the Elan and also at places like Ballingham and, far far away, at Glaslyn. Most of these fish have escaped from pools and there are not many of them about; those caught are usually big ones.

The Wye is a poor river for sea-trout and no one really knows the reason. Until fairly recently it was held that sea-trout favoured the shorter rivers and that was why they were so frequently found in large numbers in some of the Welsh rivers.We now know that sea-trout occur in considerable numbers in some Russian rivers which are as long or longer than the Wye.

To complete the trout fisherman's year we come almost full circle as the end of the season approaches and wet fly once again becomes effective. During summer the wet-fly fisherman can take a lot of stick and he would be well advised to change to dry-fly fishing. In September, though, he should do much better. Concentrate now on slightly easier water than that fished during the summer. The edges of streams and tails of pools are usually excellent although this varies. The change is subtle rather than abrupt and you will still catch trout in some rough places.

Flies for this time of year are more or less the same as those used during the rest of the season; Olive Dun, Greenwell, Pheasant Tail and Invicta and you can still use the familiar March Brown. Incidentally, the Invicta is a fairly heavily-dressed fly and yet it is really successful on the Wye.

PART 2
COARSE FISHING

Described in at least one angling paper as 'Britain's premier coarse-fishing river' there can be no doubt that the Wye offers unique opportunities for superlative fishing over much of its length. Chub, dace and pike abound and roach and perch are increasing yearly with plenty of grayling in the upper reaches.

The Wye is a clean, almost unpolluted river, its course being largely rural passing few large centres of population. There have been pollution problems in the past, particularly near Hereford, but now action has been taken to treat discharges. The pollution problem throughout the country is not an easy one to solve due to the very large sums of money involved. Fortunately, as we get more enlightened, we realise that rivers like the Wye are an essential part of life, providing recreation in superb country and relaxation from day-to-day pressures. People have been demanding that action be taken and anglers are in the forefront of this campaign.

Fishermen on the Wye, both for game and coarse fish, are now showing a considerable amount of understanding of each other's ideas and skills. It requires just as much technique to take low-water summer roach as it does to take a shy, low-water salmon and more and more coarse fishermen are taking to the pleasures of fly fishing, a most deadly way of catching many kinds of fish. Once the salmon season has ended, and in some cases during it, many coarse fishermen get permission to fish some of the finest salmon stretches on the river for coarse fish. Long may this cooperation continue and increase because it can do nothing but good for all forms of fishing and conservation.

It is a combination of geographic good fortune, watchfulness and commonsense which enables the Wye to appear in the headlines so often with fine catches of coarse fish. In 1976, for example, a Birmingham angler took 87lb 9oz in a contest, mostly chub and dace with chub up to 3½lb. The second place was 51lb 11½oz. There have been numerous bags of over 60lb since then and the prospects are apparently unlimited. Whether contest fishing, specimen hunting or simply fishing quietly at the water's side, there is plenty of room for you on the Wye.

If you do not live near the river you can ring Hereford 55333 for a pre-recorded message giving conditions and prospects for the river.

9
Chub

The chub is one of the mainstays of coarse fishing on the Wye and chub and dace are the two most frequently-caught fish. Chub are found in large numbers throughout most of the Wye system, with the exception of the upper reaches. 63lb 6oz of chub were caught by one angler in the 1972 Wye Championship and numerous bags of 32 to 40lb are reported from many parts of the river. A 5lb specimen is not unusual and fish of over 7lb have been taken. Below Monmouth 12 chub to 6¼lb with a total weight of 50lb have been reported and wherever you go on the main fishing stations on the Wye you will catch good chub. Particular attention should be paid to the Hay/Glasbury areas, Ross to Monmouth, the Lugg and Monnow.

Thick-shouldered, heavy-lipped and floating watchfully in the quieter deeper streams, the chub is worthy of the close attention of the angler. You will often see big chub sunning themselves in summer and when things get really hot and the river low and clear, they like nothing better than to shelter under the shade of overhanging trees and bushes. When disturbed there is something almost sinister in the manner in which they seem to fade away. The trout makes a panic-stricken bolt for shelter when frightened, while the chub often just sinks lower in the water into shady, more protected, water. As I have already indicated, there are plenty of big Wye chub and you need a powerful rod of 11 to 12ft with a good all-through action to deal with them. There is often a lot of weed in the Wye in summer and chub are frequently in close proximity to it. When he realises he is in trouble the first thing the chub will do is to get his head down and bolt straight into the weed and if you are using a fast tip-action rod you may not be able to stop him. Once he is in the long water ranunculus, which occurs in so many places on the Wye, your chances of getting him to the net are obviously much reduced and the encounter could easily end in a break.

If you do get caught up in weed and it is possible to move downstream try a long steady sidestrain and try to pull the fish downwards out of the weed. The natural reaction, when a fish is weeded, is to try to heave him out of it but a moment's thought will show how dangerous this is. The weed is often several feet long and very heavy and you also have the weight of the water pushing against it as well as the resistance of the fish, which will be quite happy to stay where it is. When applying pressure from downstream you are, at least, working in the direction of flow of the current and the lighter-moving ends of the weed. But act quickly because, if you give him time to burrow through the fronds you really are in trouble and may well lose a fine specimen.

Hooks should be about size 6 to 8 because the chub has a large mouth and big baits are frequently used. Always buy good-quality hooks: it's cheaper in the long run. For trotting a bait or rolling a light leger and freelining, I prefer a centrepin reel because I like working directly off the drum. However, I accept that the majority of anglers use only fixed-spool reels, and very successfully too. However, in my opinion it is a great pity that more anglers do not try free-running centrepins because they do have advantages of their own over the ubiquitous fixed spool.

For general chub fishing, when after shoal chub and in conditions which are not too weedy, a 5lb line should be sufficient, but when after specimen fish I should not hesitate to use a 7lb line. The lighter line may possibly be an advantage in places like the lower Lugg and club waters which get heavily fished but there are plenty of stretches on the Wye which are less popular and where the number of tickets is restricted. In these places light lines are quite unnecessary and, if anything, a disadvantage.

A shoal of chub nearly always contains fish of approximately the same size, although there may be one or two bigger specimens in the best position within the shoal. The best position, that is, for taking whatever food is coming down to the shoal. Bigger chub are by nature, and of necessity, much more solitary and they are found singly or in very small numbers. They are older and the survivors from shoals of a couple of years ago and the fact that they have survived means that they will be more difficult to catch now. Fortunately, under normal conditions, the chub seldom loses his appetite however big he gets; in fact he needs to eat more to support his bulk.

The problem with catching big chub is that they frequently take up positions which make it very difficult to get at them and the average and less persistent angler may be quite happy to pass by these places and concentrate on spots where he knows he is likely to get sport of some kind. When after really big chub you can have a lot of blank days before the sudden exciting moment arrives when you get a real thump of a bite. When this happens you will be very grateful for your heavier line and strong rod during the next couple of minutes.

There is no doubt that chub will, at sometime or another, take almost anything and fine fish have been caught on virtually all of the baits used on the Wye for all fish. For example, my own best chub so far, a fish of just over 5¼lb was caught when spinning for salmon with a prawn that was more than 4in long. That chub took with a typical thump, a much stronger take than I have had from a lot of salmon, and he put up a good fight even on the strong salmon-spinning kit. Although chub will certainly take these unusual baits, the most regularly successful for really big chub are undoubtedly lobworm, cheese, breadcrust and wasp grub. Spinning with a gold Mepps can also be good.

One of my favourite chub spots used to be a couple of miles below Ross where a small drain trickled into the river. Here the water deepened close to the bank and slid quietly beneath overhanging bushes. It was typical of places I have previously mentioned which are rather difficult to fish. In the summer there was a fine growth of tall venomous nettles. Brambles added to the enjoyment and when you finally got to the water's edge the overhanging branches dipped into the water and made things quite tricky. I was not anxious to do all the work for someone else's benefit so I did not cut out the area. I sidled gently through the undergrowth so that when I had finished fishing the place still looked almost untouched.

In this place my favourite method was to use a smooth-drilled bullet with a good-sized hole and of sufficient weight just to hold bottom comfortably until the rod point was lifted. The

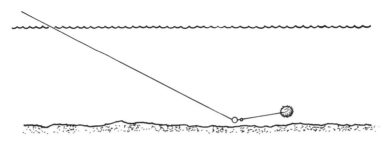

One of the best ways of exploring likely chub lies is to leger with a drilled bullet. The bullet should be stopped, by a shot, about 14 inches from the hook. Choose a bullet which is just heavy enough to hold bottom. The bait can then be made to explore the swim by a gentle lift of the rod top

bullet was stopped by a shot 12 to 14in from the hook. Bait was usually a fairly large piece of crust. The bait was swung out and allowed to hold bottom, then it was steered slowly down to the inviting depths below the branches by moving the rod point across the surface of the water and lifting occasionally to raise the bullet off the bottom. In this way the bait could be allowed to swing in the current for about thirty seconds, just off the bottom, in each halt until it was well down into the spot which, from experience, I knew was likely to be the best taking place. If nothing happened the line was then reeled quietly in and the bait renewed. Bites were nearly always firm and bitter experience taught me that it was necessary to get the fish out from underneath those branches as quickly as I could.

There is nothing better than using a bait in which you have faith and while most of my chub fishing in that spot was done with breadcrust I have little doubt that someone else would have done just as well with cheese or any other substantial chub bait.

This spot proved to be excellent for winter chub as well but as the water becomes colder chub get much less impetuous and take more time examining and sampling a bait before pouching it. Thus the bait has to stay on the hook a long time and still remain presentable, so in winter I prefer lobworms and cheese.

The kind of place I have been talking about occurs frequently in one form or another along the Wye and a great many of them are rarely fished because of the difficulty in getting at them. Take my word for it, the effort, scratches and stings are well worth enduring.

If you have no wish to suffer the discomforts which can be an integral part of specimen hunting there is still plenty of good chub fishing to be had on the Wye. School chub of about 2lb abound and the methods already described are very successful with these fish. At different times chub will feed at all levels in the river from the bottom to the surface and during the summer they can usually be tempted at one of these levels and with at least one of the usual baits. I previously mentioned using a drilled bullet with breadcrust but a lighter and much more sensitive method, when summer fishing for school chub, is to use a short loop of monofilament over the line, secured by several swan shot. A single shot, about 12in from the hook, stops the loop from going down to the hook and leaves the line free to pass easily through the loop when a fish takes the bait. Worms, cheese and paste are all good baits for this method.

To illustrate what I mean about catching chub at all levels in the water, I have often seen a fisherman catching chub with a leger while, just along the bank, another angler is float fishing successfully. In the most recent instance, the float fisherman was holding back at the end of the swim to take bites when the bait was quite near the surface.

Sometimes, however, only one method seems to be really successful so it is advisable always to carry a selection of baits and be prepared to use different methods until one is found which is readily accepted by the fish. As a contrast to legered crust an exciting alternative is to surface fish a large piece of crust beneath bankside trees and bushes which overhang medium-depth water or to use the same technique in streams between weed-beds.

In many places the Wye is a broad shallow river during the summer months with many areas of extensive weed growth which breaks up the river into weed-locked lakes with occasional passages between the luxuriant growths. These places can be completely unfishable from the bank but there is no reason why the coarse fisherman should not put on a pair of waders and move quietly out amongst the weed-beds where he should get some fine fishing.

Keep as far back from the clear channels as you can and swim the crust down the edges of the streams quite close to the weed. This can be a deadly method, particularly towards evening, and fish will come boldly to the bait as long as your approach is cautious, preferably with the sun in front of you so that your shadow does not fall on the water.

Wipe over the used part of the line with a fly floatant liquid and pay particular attention to the couple of yards before the bait. When the line stays on the surface you are in direct contact and can strike firmly when needed with a minimum of disturbance. Because the bait is on the surface you often see the first movement of the fish as it comes to take it, but this is one of the instances when you should not be in too much of a hurry. Give the fish a chance to turn down with the bait before you tighten otherwise you can easily pull the bait away from it.

If you do not wish to wade and the weed growth is not too troublesome you can still cover an enormous amount of water with float tackle. It may be necessary to use a composite float, such as cork and quill, which can carry a fair amount of lead and make casting easier.

If you are not sure of the depth do not put on a hook immediately but add sufficient shot to really cock the float near the bottom of the line. Set the float at what you think is the correct depth and after making one or two casts you should have a very good idea of what the true general depth is. When you start fishing, begin with the bait just off the bottom but if, after a little time, this brings no results try shortening the depth and bringing the bait up nearer midwater.

If you want to use a groundbait use something like bread and bran, weighted with stones to ensure that it gets to the bottom quickly. Add a few samples of the hook bait to the groundbait. As in all cases when using groundbait remember that the idea is to get the fish interested and not to give them a good feed. In slow water a looser mix can be made than would be advisable in fast water where the current would quickly whip the particles away.

If you happen to catch the chub just as a hint of colour is coming into the water, together with a rise in level, you are unlikely to go far wrong. For a few hours the whole river seems to come alive with fish feeding everywhere and at such times you get a good idea of just how many fish there are in any stretch of water. Pike and big chub will splash around near the surface after

The river is best known among coarse anglers for its superb chub fishing. This 3½lb specimen was taken from a swim near the bridge at Ross-on-Wye

fry and small fish and there are rises everywhere as all sorts of fish feed on the floating debris.

However, if the rise continues and the water gets dirtier and faster, it becomes much harder to catch fish. A summer flood on the Wye can leave the water high and coloured for a week or ten days although the level may never have approached that of a spring flood. The Ithon, Lugg and Llynfi are the main culprits and it can be like fishing a different river if you happen to be just above the confluence of one of these tributaries with the main river as opposed to just below it. If you have to fish high water try to fish backwaters and sheltered banks which do not get the full force of the current. As the water begins to drop and clear, fishing will often improve dramatically again.

Dapping can be a good method of taking these summer chub when you have overhanging bankside bushes. Dapping is best done with as little lead as possible and with the bait hanging virtually straight down from the rod. Use two or three small shot, as required, rather than one big one, and space them a couple of inches apart. One big shot tends to swing more and drag the bait across the surface, which is not wanted. The idea is to gently drop the bait onto the water and keep it there, almost suspended on the surface with no line falling onto the water. Let the bait move gently down with the current or drift around unhindered in likely holes. The take will usually be definite and firm but give the chub a moment to take the bait down before tightening. As the bait is hanging on a rather taut line be ready to drop the rod point as soon as a fish takes so that he feels no resistance.

Summer chub also love a spun bait and I have had great sport with a gold Mepps. If you use a light spinning rod and fixed-spool reel with 5lb line and attach a ball-bearing swivel just over 1ft from the bait, you have a perfect spinning kit for Wye chub. Keep the bait working at about mid-water level and fish the medium-depth streams. Where the current is fairly strong cast across the stream and allow the bait to swing around without winding until it gets below you. If the bait is being worked well by the water you will feel it throbbing through the line. If you wind too quickly you will simply draw the bait through the surface film of water and although you will catch odd chub this is

Wading on the Upper Wye can be extremely dangerous. The wise angler moves very cautiously

not the best way to use the lure.

When chub are rising but cannot be reached with a fly, a bait such as a Mepps can be used very successfully near the surface. Note the point of the rise and get upstream of it. Then cast across and allow the bait to swing around towards the position where you last saw the rise. Keep winding as the bait swings around to keep it well up near the surface. If your movements have not disturbed it the chub will carry on rising and you can work gradually down until you are certain that the bait has actually covered the rising area. The bait will often be taken with a wallop. Always remember to start well above the fish otherwise you are likely to drop the bait right on top of it. Occasionally this results in an immediate take but it is much more likely to scare the fish.

I have always thought that one of the most enjoyable methods of catching chub is with an artificial fly. They will take a fly freely and it is great fun to cast directly to a rising fish or to cover likely areas where one thinks chub should be. Generally speaking, chub like a good stream and the best fish are usually found where the broken water finishes and the deeper water begins. You will often pick up good chub at the edges of these streams and, if you are able, cover the tail of the stream as well where it opens out. The channels between weed-beds and the weed-locked lakes which I mentioned before for crust fishing are ideal for dry-fly fishing but you do have to be cautious when fishing these areas. The current through them is frequently slow and the surface of the water extremely smooth. Careless wading will send a warning ripple across many yards of water and this may stop the fish rising for a while. When a chub takes, tighten firmly but not hastily. If you really heave the hook into a big chub you will very probably break on the strike.

Early morning and towards evening are the ideal times for this game. During the heat of a summer's day the fish tend to become lethargic and it is by no means unusual to catch only small chub until conditions improve towards evening.

Incidentally, do be especially careful if you are not used to wading. On many of the big Wye flats it is very easy to be tempted further and further out by rising fish and it is easy to make progress when you can see the bottom clearly. However, it may be a different matter if you find yourself out in the middle of the river in failing light. When you turn around to head for the bank you can sometimes see only the surface of the water and everything else looks black. It can be quite unnerving to feel for the ridges and shallow spots which you could see quite easily on the way out. As for wading on the rocky upper river the answer is simple: wherever it can be avoided do not wade at all. The upper Wye is in some places just about the most slippery and dangerous place I know for wading. Ordinary rubber soles give no grip whatsoever and the only kind that gives any sort of security is a thick felt sole. I can tell you from experience that it is not funny to find yourself sliding uncontrollably towards six or eight feet of fast-moving rock-strewn water. In any case, as far as the coarse fisherman is concerned, much of the upper river is considerably narrower than the middle and lower reaches with quick streams and rocky areas interspersed between the smoother, slower-flowing places. In these areas wading is quite unnecessary and as long as the bankside growth of bushes and trees allows, the water can normally be covered comfortably from the bank. Weed growth too is less of a problem in this faster-flowing part of the river.

When dry-fly fishing for chub any fly rod will do at a push, but where there is a choice, use one with a stiffer action than the softer one usually associated with wet-fly fishing. The traditional fly for chub is a Buzzy Palmer but this is by no means necessary or even advisable. With low clear summer water, a frequent problem on the Wye, I should much prefer to go chub fishing with a somewhat heavier dressed, but otherwise standard, hackled trout fly.

For wet-fly fishing concentrate on the streams where there is a good current and not less than about three feet of water. Here again, any of the larger hackled trout wet flies are good as are sea-trout flies, particularly with red and silver on them. My own favourite, head and shoulders above the rest for the Wye, is an Invicta.

If you can be bothered to set up a minnow trap in the sunny shallows you can catch fine chub by fishing them live. Hook them through the top lip and suspend them with a buoyant float to search eddies and medium-depth edges of streams. A big shot will probably be needed to keep the minnow down in the water. Personally, I prefer using deadbaits fished sink and draw. Use a baiting needle to thread the minnow onto the line and pull the line out at the side, near the tail. A small treble hook is added and one point pushed into the side of the bait and a small bullet or a couple of swan shot will be needed on the nose of the bait to make it sink head first. A fixed-spool reel is perfect for this game. The bait is tossed out across a likely, preferably weed-free, area and allowed to sink to the bottom. It is left there a few seconds then the rod is raised high to draw the bait to the surface when it is allowed to slip freely to the bottom again. Each time this is done the bait comes a little nearer until it can be lifted from the water. Apart from chub you may pick up an odd perch with this method and there is always the chance of a pike. If a pike takes hold, the shot may give the line some protection but on several occasions I have had the line cut as clean as a whistle when the bait has been taken by a pike.

During the winter, chub leave the quicker streams and retire to deeper slower water and this is where you have to look for them. They can become rather lethargic but shy and often slower to take a bait than would seem possible with such greedy fish.

Maggots and casters can be used from 26 October and many Wye fishermen use them to the exclusion of all other baits. In my opinion this is a mistake and I often think that bigger better fish are taken on baits like lobworm, cheese or crust. With these winter chub it is by no means unusual for them virtually to ignore a bait for some time even though it is quite close to them. For this reason use a bait which will stay on the hook well and, preferably, leger it. Both suggestions will considerably increase the chance of getting in to good fish.

A drilled bullet or link leger is excellent for winter chubbing. Stop the bullet or link about 10in from the bait and if you use a bullet make sure that there is a good-sized hole in it. Whatever method of weighting the bait is used it must hold the bait still and steady. At this time of year I do not like a roving leger. It is a different matter if you raise the rod point every few minutes to let the bait drop gently downstream to a new fixed position. This is perfectly acceptable and can be deadly. What seems to happen is that chub will apparently ignore a bait for some time then, if it stays in the same place, move over to inspect it. The next step is to move or nibble the bait and this can be a difficult moment for the fisherman who has to decide whether the tremblings and twitchings indicate that the fish has the bait in its mouth or is simply playing with it. To tighten too soon is to miss the fish and it requires a nice judgment to interpret exactly what is happening. On these difficult days it is advisable to hold the rod in one hand and the line in the other and to keep the line fairly taut. Be ready to drop the rod point if a pull comes but you feel the fish has not taken hold. This is a more sensitive method than leaving the rod in a rest and the fish is less likely to pick up any sense of resistance. If you do miss one of these big chub you may have to change to a completely different bait or even move elsewhere to get any further offers. It is not always like this though: sometimes the fish will take the bait firmly and other times there is a combination of both kinds of take.

I was only an observer to what seemed likely to end up as one of the best catches of good chub seen on the Wye in recent years, but it was quite an education. It was a good November day near Hay and the fisherman was using a drilled bullet and a lump of cheese. The river had a fair flow on but it was clear and cold. The method was to spend no more than twenty minutes in one spot, dropping in the bait quite close to the bank, then working it down into a hole by lifting the bait every couple of minutes for the current to move it. The first fish took strongly enough but the second one, from the same spot, was much more crafty. The line dithered and bobbed a few times then things went quiet for a while until a good pull came. That was the end of the fun in that place so we moved on elsewhere. The pattern was much the same as far as the bites were concerned, some good and some tentative. Only one chub came from this spot but a further two came from the next hole. That fisherman really knew what he was doing. He knew the water as well and everything was going right for him. Those five chub weighed upwards of four pounds each. He was still going strong when I left him but I never found out what the final score was.

10
Dace

Dace are found in large numbers throughout the whole of the Wye with the exception of the extreme upper reaches of the river. It is not just numbers that make dace fishing so interesting on the Wye because specimens of about a pound are caught quite often. This pretty little fish with its dark back and silver-shaded sides is a fascinating quarry. Sometimes, if there is a tinge of colour in the water, you cannot go wrong and great bags can be made. But at other times when the water is low and clear and the sun hard and bright the position is very different. At such times dace become very choosy and you may have great difficulty in catching just a few.

The Wye is a wonderful river to write about as well as to fish and it is very easy to allow oneself to get carried away when describing the fishing. However, once again, the records speak for themselves. A bag of 120 dace was made by one angler at Bodenham while another took 36lb 6oz at Skenfrith, on the Monnow. 48lb 3½oz, nearly all dace, has been reported from the lower Wye and 120 dace, weighing 40lb, have been caught at Hoarwithy. 140 dace were credited to one fisherman at Llanstephan. In an *Angling Times* League fixture in 1972 at Bigsweir the first three teams recorded weights of 64lb 3½oz, 63lb 0¾oz and 32lb 6½oz, mostly dace. Fish of a pound or more have been reported from as far apart as Glasbury, the lower Lugg, Ross, Bigsweir, Hay and Monmouth.

The Wye is a very clean river and this is one of the main reasons why there are so many dace about. For much of the year the river is often clear and dace will be busy in the summer on the sparkling shallows and in the generally quicker-moving water. In the winter they retire to deeper, more sedate waters, but they do like some current.

The usual choice of rod for dace fishing will be hollow glass or carbon fibre, 12ft or a little longer in length. The vast majority of anglers will use a fixed-spool reel for all of their fishing but there is still a very good case to be made for the use of a free running centrepin reel for some float fishing, particularly where there is no need to cast long distances. Incidentally, the bite of a dace is quick and seldom repeated so the rod, whatever the material, should have a brisk tip action. A slow, through-action rod can miss a lot of bites and produce a lot of frustration. When dace fishing on the Wye I reckon a 2lb line is as fine as you will need. There may be some heavily fished club waters where the fish are slightly more cautious but, generally speaking, Wye dace are not so persecuted that ridiculously fine lines are required to deceive them. In addition, there is always the chance of finding oneself attached to one of the larger fish in the river and when this happens you do at least stand a reasonable chance with a 2lb line. As long as you do not break in the strike a 2lb line can kill large fish and take a lot of punishment. I know it has been done but I should hate to find myself playing a 4lb chub on a 1lb line when it need never have happened.

This business of fishing a very fine line with tiny hooks has, in my opinion, been very much overdone. If you are fishing close in, it is just as important, if not more important, to move quietly and unobtrusively and to keep off the skyline. Dace are quick, shy little fish and thoughtless heavy movements can scare them off or at best send the shoal further out into the stream. I should very much prefer to go after dace with a 4lb line and 12 hook in a place where the water was completely undisturbed than I would try my luck with the finest tackle available in a badly disturbed spot. Again, if the water is heavily fished you could go down to a 16 hook but that is quite small enough for anywhere I know on the Wye.

Maggots are undoubtedly the most popular Wye bait for dace but casters are also widely used. At present the byelaws state that maggots, grubs or larvae may not be used between 14 March and 26 October in almost all of the tributaries and the whole of the Wye. A slight relaxation of the maggot ban is being sought.

During the summer months, when maggots are not allowed, a small fragment of flake or a tiny worm can be taken quite freely. Because the dace is a shoaling fish groundbait is normally used to attract the fish into the area of operations. Use finely ground breadcrumbs with just a very little of the hook bait buried in it if the swim you are working on cannot be reached with loose feed alone. The well-worn phrase, a little and often, applies to groundbaiting because too much is as harmful as too little.

The texture of the mix may need adjusting to suit conditions in different places. It is no good heaving in a couple of balls of very light-texture bait in a spot where there is a fair depth of quick water because the mixture will be broken up and whipped away before the dace see it properly. On the other hand, neither is it advisable to use a heavy mix in a shallow, gentle current. Bran mixed with the bait gives a texture which tends to break up more slowly, and this can be useful under certain circumstances. Don't forget that if great balls of groundbait come hammering in on top of dace in clear summer water they will move elsewhere. Under these difficult conditions, try to use loose feed only, frequently but sparingly. When you start getting bites the shoal is obviously interested. Now comes the really difficult part. If you give them too little feed they will lose interest and move off and if you give them too much they won't bother with the hook bait.

One other important point about groundbait is the need to decide just where to put it in order to attract the fish into the spot where you want them. If the current is strong it will have to go in some distance upstream to avoid being swept away and wasted on fish many yards downstream. If you place the groundbait too far above you the shoal will move past towards the source of the food. If you start getting bites and then they fall off this might be the reason. If you suspect this is so, move quietly upstream about ten yards and begin fishing again, using a little loosefeed only.

When float fishing for dace remember that you are after a small, delicate fish so keep the rig as light as conditions will allow. For fishing fairly close in, a quill or stick float is fine. Make sure that it is properly shotted so that only the minimum shows above the surface. This way the float is better able to indicate the light fleeting bite of the dace than it would be with a large amount of the float showing.

If the shoals are well out into the stream a larger-bodied float

A fighting winter dace is swung to hand from the river near Whitney

will be needed, partly to aid casting but also to steer a more regular course when some distance away from the angler. The small floats are easily pulled off course by the slight resistance of the line and will work in towards the bank. The bigger float has more of an area to resist this.

Whatever float is decided on, the problem of distributing the shot can often cause trouble. If dace are taking the bait on the drop and most of the shot are near the float, to make it cock quickly, the fish can be in, take the bait and be gone with nothing to indicate that a bite has been missed, until the line is pulled in. Dace can be infuriating when they get up to this trick but the problem can often be overcome by putting one or more small shot within 6 or 8in of the bait. This will get the bait quickly down to its fishing level and nearly all types of bite will then register, whether as a dipping or rising of the float or a deviation from its normal course or speed. Even this is not infallible because dace can quite easily move at the same pace as the bait and delicately remove it without moving the bottom shot or altering the speed of the line. When this happens nothing shows. If you are fishing a place where there is a fair amount of water to choose from, don't waste too much time in one spot if fish do not show up. Where there is plenty of room I think it is better to change position quietly and begin fishing again about twenty yards away rather than resort to long trotting. This tends to be a less efficient method of catching dace, except in expert hands, than the methods already described.

The longer the trot the more difficult it becomes to see exactly what is happening to the float and many of the tiny teasing bites will go unnoticed. The longer line also makes it much more difficult to strike sharply enough which is often so necessary for the consistent hooking of dace.

We have been talking so far about ordinary summer fishing when the water may be low but the conditions are not severely testing. When there is a period of prolonged low water and the temperature is high and the sky bright dace can become very shy indeed. It is essential for the bait to behave naturally. Very light, on-the-drop fishing can be good, otherwise try a small float and light shotting, using the heaviest shot at the top and the smallest at the bottom. Current speeds will be less as the level of the water drops and it is helpful at such times not to have any shot nearer than 12in to the bait. To give yourself the best chance try to concentrate your fishing in the two periods of early morning and evening when fishing conditions should be better and the fish more cooperative. There is one consolation. A dozen good dace caught at times like this are worth more than a large number caught much more easily when conditions are good.

On the Wye there are plenty of good clean gravel fords where dace abound and they can be tackled in these places with an adaptation of the trout fisherman's upstream worming technique. The float is dispensed with and a minimum of lead shot is used, probably dust shot, spaced from about 6in from the bait and sufficient to barely hold bottom. The bait travels downstream, tapping the bottom and moving more slowly than the current. The secret lies in getting the amount of lead right. Too much and the bait is held up all the time; too little and the bait tends to move too quickly. The bait can be fished upstream or downstream and while bites are detected much more easily when fishing downstream hooking is much safer when fishing upstream. Strike at any slight stoppage or hesitation of the line. Ideally this method is best used when you are able to wade and cover a lot of water but it is a different and interesting alternative to float fishing and worth bearing in mind when a suitable place is seen.

One other method for summer dace must be mentioned and that is fly fishing. Any light fly outfit will do and it is best to use simple hackle flies which float better than the winged patterns. Any of the regular trout patterns such as Greenwell's Glory, March Brown or Pheasant Tail are ideal and they should be fished in the shallow- to medium-depth streams or wherever you see dace rising. If you have never done any fly fishing this is the perfect way to start and it is very exciting to see the dimpling rise as the dace comes to the fly. You have to strike quickly, just as you do when float fishing. Again, although fly fishing often benefits from being used in conjunction with wading there are hundreds of places on the Wye where grand sport can be had from the bank. Provided you keep off the skyline, wading is quite unnecessary in these places and much better avoided.

In the winter the dace move into deeper quieter water. Float fishing with maggots or casters is by far the most popular method on the Wye and large numbers of dace are caught in this way throughout the autumn and winter months. As winter water heights and temperatures become established the dace are less inclined to move so far afield and once the shoal has been contacted good sport can often be had. In contrast to their summer location in the shallows dace will now be found mostly at or below middle water and I like to shot to get the rig fishing properly, float cocked and bait at fishing depth, as quickly as possible. To do this have one shot, about a BB, within 8in of the bait. Vary the level of the bait by altering the float which is usually more successful at this time of year than fishing on the drop.

Another good method, especially in the winter, is a light link leger. Make a loop of monofilament over the line and secure it with enough shot to hold bottom where you intend fishing. Keep the link away from the bait with a stop shot about 8in from the hook. Use enough lead to keep the bait still but no more. A virtually stationary bait is frequently more successful during cold conditions and this is a method which accounts for some of the best dace. (Try a small worm as well as maggots from time to time.)

The light leger can, of course, be used very effectively in the summer as well. Fished to the edges of good currents or, on hot days, under the cover of trees or bushes it can, again, produce some of the best dace fishing; less in numbers perhaps but better in size.

II

Eels and Elvers

Most people know of the enormous numbers of elvers which enter the Severn each spring. It is not so generally known that there is a large run of elvers in the Wye as well and although they are not fished for on the same commercial scale as on the Severn, elver fishing on the Wye is still a flourishing pastime. In an effort to gain some information as to the extent of the elver fishing in the river, anyone who wants to go after elvers now has to obtain a licence before doing so. At the moment there is no charge for the licence.

After entering the river and eventually spreading almost throughout its entire length, the elvers settle down to a period of seven or more years in the river before they start their return migration to the sea. Before they become fully mature, young eels are dark brown or olive on the back and creamy white or yellow underneath. When fully mature and ready for migration, eels turn silver.

As might be expected many fine eels are caught on the Wye and most years specimens in excess of 3lb are taken. A 4½-pounder came from Wilton, below Ross, and a 5lb 4oz eel has been caught in the Monnow. Just to show how widespread these big eels are a fine one of 4¼lb was caught in the upper Lugg in 1974.

There must be considerably larger eels than these in the river but, again, there are not many fishermen seriously intent on catching them. An eel specialist is a rarity and the fine eels reported are mostly taken by fishermen legering generally with worms in the daytime. This is not the way to go after a specimen eel.

A dead bleak, minnow or gudgeon is likely to be the best bait followed by a strip of herring or a skinned section out of a small eel. Another quite useful bait is a couple of big lobworms. No doubt the apparent difficulty in obtaining suitable bait at the right time has something to do with the small number of big eel fishermen but it shouldn't be much of a problem. Minnows, for example, will congregate in the sunny shallows right at the bankside and if you do not have a proper trap, put down a wide-necked net with a few scraps of bread or worms on it. When the fish gather over the net to inspect the goodies lift smartly and you should have a few baits to be going on with. Stirring the bottom just above the trap will sometimes help to attract the quarry. A bottle trap can be good on some occasions. Use a clear wine bottle with a dome in the base and tap out the tip of the dome to allow access. I find it best not to use a cork in the neck of the bottle but to tie a small piece of plastic over it, quite tightly. Make a few holes in the plastic to let some water dribble through the bottle and all should be well. Bait up in the same manner as with a net, scraps of bread or worm.

Fresh baits are best so the ideal way is to keep them alive in a bucket until an hour or so before they are needed, when they can be tapped on the head and put in a suitable tin with damp moss. Remember too, that if you catch more bait fish than you need they can be kept for months between layers of rough salt in a jar. You then always have baits available should a sudden opportunity to fish arise.

Whatever bait is being used I strongly recommend a finished length of 12 to 14in of 15lb breaking strain single wire, such as Alasticum, below a ballbearing swivel. The line should not be less than 15lb breaking strain. If this seems heavy remember that you are likely to be fishing in comparative darkness and may have to bully a big strong eel out of weed or away from a known snag without the benefit of really seeing what you are doing. The rod should be powerful and not less than 9ft 6in and I like a simple centrepin reel with a good strong check.

I do not cast far when eeling but simply draw off some line and let it drop on a white-sheet 'landing ground' before swinging out the bait. Don't move about at this stage, to avoid treading on the line. By all means use a fixed-spool reel if you prefer but beware of loose coils of line which can easily be picked up in the dark by the bale arm and wrapped around most unlikely places. Big eels are not contacted very often even on the Wye and it is something of a tragedy to contact a really big one only to find that the reel has jammed or the line has been seriously weakened.

I much prefer good-quality single hooks, about size 6, for eel fishing. Trebles are used but the eel has a small mouth and I prefer to rely on a single. The bait itself is rather bulky and a treble can cause leverage problems.

To mount a deadbait, pass a baiting needle through the mouth and out at the vent, pulling the bend of the hook snugly into the side of the mouth. Make up several baits in preparation for an evening's fishing and have them conveniently ready in a large tin, preferably with some damp moss around them.

Use only enough lead to keep the bait still on the bottom and if it will hold without lead, so much the better. It may be necessary to puncture the air bladder of the bait to ensure it stays quietly on the bottom. The idea is to keep the bait motionless on the bottom but to give as little resistance as possible to an eel when it takes. A light well-drilled bullet stopped by a shot about a foot from the bait is fine or you could use a link leger.

For lobworms thread one up the shank of the hook and hang another over the point. When using lobworms I think it is best to bring the lead just a little nearer the bait to ensure it stays anchored. Keep a deadbait on the small side. This does not seem to affect the size of eel which can be caught, in fact it probably does the reverse. As long as the bait is dropped into a good spot an eel will take and swallow a comparatively small bait much more quickly and easily than a large one.

Groundbaiting can certainly help to attract good eels. You can either use minced fish, or herring which is excellent because of its oily texture, or you can lower a pierced can filled with offal or fish close to where you are going to start operations.

A period of warm settled weather offers the best conditions for specimen eel hunting and warm summer nights are the best time. If there are the signs of a slight rise in the level of water with a hint of colour from rain upstream, eels are almost sure to be in a hunting mood.

If you must fish during the daytime concentrate on the deeper slower tails of streams or holes with some movement. Bright

The river at Llanstephan, mid-Wales (*John Tarlton*)

sunshine is bad for this game and you are unlikely to get much
success with big eels. But from dusk onwards they move up on
to shallower places with quite a reasonable current and in suitable
places you will find them in two or three feet of water. Below
the mouth of a ditch or drain is often a fine place. Smaller eels
congregate in good feeding places in considerably less depth than
this and I have frequently heard them right under the bank in
about a foot of water busily sucking flies from overhanging

branches. I have never caught a really large eel in as shallow water as this and I suspect that they are not as bold as the smaller ones, hence the reason for their survival.

It is advisable to have a careful look along the river bank in daylight to choose suitable places for night fishing. The bottom should be free from heavy weed growth which makes the bait more difficult to find and it should only be necessary to cast a short distance.

If you leave the rod in a rest it can be helpful to fold a piece of white paper and place it over the line between the reel and first ring. Make sure that the line is free to run when an eel takes and before you can pick up the rod. It is in the first couple of seconds that firm resistance may well cause an eel to leave the bait.

The only difficulty comes in timing the strike. Depending on the size of the bait and the state of the eel's appetite, more or less time will have to be given before tightening. Resist the temptation to act until the twitches and plucks have turned into a steady pull which indicates that the eel has really got the bait in its mouth and is moving off with it. When you do strike give a good haul on the rod to move the eel off the bottom. If you don't do this and there are snags close by you can still get into trouble even with a 15lb line.

It is also helpful to choose a spot for fishing where the bank is low and without too much vegetation. If an otherwise ideal spot is spoiled by tall grass or nettles, cut them. Cover the site close to the water with a large old white sheet and secure the edges with metal tent pegs. This enables you to see much more easily what you are doing when you bring in an eel than you possibly could if you tried to do it on bankside growth. Keep a piece of dry rough cloth or sacking handy to get a good grip on the eel immediately behind the head.

The easiest way to despatch an eel is to put your foot on its 'neck' and sink the blade of a sharp knife into the base of the skull. The white sheet is a great help at this time and you will be able to deal much more confidently with the situation. Keep hold of the line with one hand while you use the knife with the other. This keeps the hands apart and reduces the risk of injuring yourself because it is easy to make a slip in the excitement of the moment. You can get a nasty bite from a big eel, so be careful. I cut the wire with a small pair of pliers immediately below the swivel, put the eel in a sack and tie the mouth of the sack before putting on a new bait. Ensure that the new wire is wound tightly and a sufficient number of times around itself after being passed through the eye of the swivel. Give it a good pull to test it, just in case.

I always carry a good lamp on these outings but seldom use it, reserving it for some emergency such as a tangle or breakage. Whatever you do don't let the light get on the water if you do make a habit of using one. It takes a little time after the use of artificial light for the eyes to get accustomed to the comparative dark again and as there is invariably a glimmer of light in the sky on a summer night I prefer to do without a lamp.

There is undoubtedly enormous potential for this type of fishing on the Wye and if you are prepared to wait until dusk before making a start you should get some first-rate sport.

12
Grayling

These lovely fish have dark-greyish backs with softly iridescent sides and grey lines along their bodies. They like fast-flowing streams with a gravelly bottom and in many places the Wye provides them with virtually perfect conditions. The grayling is a member of the salmon family and has the small adipose fin in front of the tail as do the salmon and trout. For some reason, and I don't think it is known, the grayling spawns around April whereas salmon and trout spawn at the end of the year. The grayling therefore is classed with coarse fish as far as its close season is concerned.

There is a good head of grayling in the upper parts of the Wye with a 3lb fish reported from the Builth area in 1974. The Hay and Glasbury areas also produce good grayling and the species can be contacted all the way downstream, in suitable places, to Monmouth. Like the trout the grayling population diminishes as we come down-stream and although they are taken occasionally at Hereford and Ross they are, in these places, a delightful bonus rather than a normal quarry. The tributaries offer the best grayling fishing, however, with the Lugg, Arrow, Llynfi and Monnow, for example, offering plenty of opportunity for good fishing. The Monnow produces some really big grayling and this is a little surprising bearing in mind that it is generally quite a slow-flowing river. Some grayling have been introduced into the river system and it is recorded that 4,000 young fish were placed in the Dore, a tributary of the Monnow, on 16 May 1882.

Grayling shoals can be seen spawning on the gravelly shallows from March to May, depending on river conditions. Again, depending on conditions, they soon regain their strength and fitness and take their places in similar streams to trout. They often give good sport in summer but it is in autumn or early winter that the grayling is at its peak. By this time the fighting qualities of the fish are beyond doubt.

Grayling can be caught on dry fly, wet fly and nymph throughout the summer and often into early winter. When autumn arrives, fishing patterns, and particularly fly-fishing patterns, tend to revert to what they were in the early part of the year and sport is frequently restricted to an hour or so either side of midday. This is not so noticeable with grayling as it is with trout but there is a tendency in that direction.

The normal trout fly-fishing kit is ideal for grayling and the usual trout flies for the Wye are perfectly acceptable to this fish. For dry fly try a March Brown, Greenwell or Pheasant Tail and, if using wet fly, a Hare's Ear or Invicta.

The grayling is a shoaling fish and this should be borne in mind when fishing for it. The trout is an individual and, within reason, you can catch one and move on a little further to catch another. With the grayling it is wiser to remember that it is the shoal rather than the individual that is the quarry. In the summer the shoal gives away its position by its collection of dimpling or, sometimes, splashy rises. The untidy rises are usually made in fairly deep water where the fish comes up from the bottom in a rush to take the fly.

When dry-fly fishing for grayling cast to the nearside edge of the shoal first to, hopefully, take a couple of fish before dropping the fly in the middle of the shoal. Grayling are not generally tackle-shy but they will react if a fish is hooked in the middle of the shoal and makes a disturbance before it is landed.

In shallow- to medium-depth water there is no great difference between the take of a grayling and a trout. Don't be afraid to set the hook fairly firmly because it is the sides of a grayling's mouth which are tender, not the roof. In deeper water the grayling does tend to come at the fly from the bottom in a rush and it often misses. You soon get used to this and once you are fairly sure where the fly is you can resist the temptation to strike at a false rise. Sometimes the fish will turn and try again but often it will go back down and you will have to recast.

In August I have often quietly waded out on to a wide swiftly moving flat near Erwood and caught half a dozen grayling without changing position. Once you have traced the shoal and they do move around quite a lot over a period, the battle is half over. If you are reasonably cautious the drop of the line and inevitable disturbance as the fly is picked from the surface do not seem to put the grayling down. The shoal will stay in the same general area for some days, or even weeks, but suddenly something happens which makes it move off elsewhere and you then have to go looking for it again. The movements are normally restricted within the limits of a large flat. Admittedly that can be a big area to search but the grayling is easier to find than the perch, which can be a most elusive quarry.

If the shoal is located but the fish are not rising try one of the small trout nymphs or a Sawyer Killer Bug. Use a floating line and be prepared to grease a part of the cast so that only the last couple of feet sink. The classic way to fish a nymph is upstream and you have to keep a very careful watch on the cast where it enters the water to spot the slight hesitation or twitch which tells the trained eye that a fish has taken. So many compromises have to be made in fishing and a very good one is to fish the nymph square across the stream. Takes are a little easier to spot, although one seldom feels the definite pluck that comes when fishing downstream, and the percentage of secure hookings is excellent.

Apart from artificial fly and nymph, grayling will freely take a trotted worm or maggot. Remember the maggot ban which at present lasts until 26 October. Caddis grubs are welcomed by grayling too. Use a 9 or 10ft rod, preferably with a quick action, and a free-running centrepin reel. You can certainly use a fixed spool if you prefer but you should give the centrepin a try first. A good quality hook, about size 12, will be fine.

The type of float used must be decided by the conditions and one's own feelings. There is at present a reaction against the traditional grayling bob and yet it does have some advantages in really shallow water. A long light quill or stick float is certainly sensitive but it is very unstable in rough shallow water and it penetrates much further below the surface than a bob. Whichever float you use it should be carefully shotted so that it responds to the gentle bite of the grayling and is clearly visible in the difficult conditions of rough foamy water. As a compromise between one of the long stick floats and a bob try one of the short balsa floats which has some of the advantages of each. They

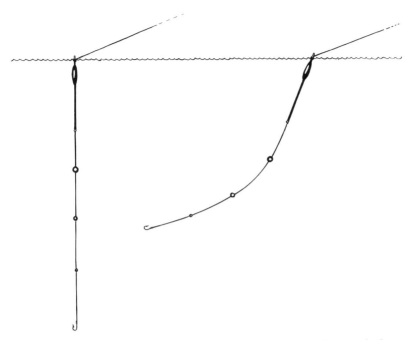

When fishing deeper water spread the shot evenly down the line, with the largest shot nearest the float. If no bites result pull the float back gently so that the bait will rise towards the surface

can be obtained about four inches long and are sensitive and quite stable.

In the really shallow places and smooth medium-flowing flats it can be productive to freeline a small worm or couple of maggots or casters. A tiny amount of shot may be needed from time to time to help casting or slow down the passage of the bait through a stream. The addition of any lead means, of course, that this is not true freelining but it is near enough for all practical purposes and the absence of a float reduces the disturbance of the water.

When using a float in the deeper places spread the shot down the line with the smaller ones nearer the bait but not nearer than about a foot. If the water varies frequently in depth, have most of the shot fairly near to the float and a dust shot only about a foot above the bait. If you hold back in the shallow water the current will carry the bait on but when you come to the deeper places let the float go and the bottom shot should be sufficient to take the bait down to the fish. This can be a very deadly and versatile method of fishing problem waters. The only alternative is to change the shotting pattern each time the bait has to fish a deep spot instead of a shallow one and vice versa.

An interesting thing about grayling is that they can be caught at most depths in the water and the presentation of the bait at one precise depth is not anywhere near as important as it can be with roach or even dace. When trotting an even medium depth make a start at about middle depth and hold back occasionally to get the bait to swing upwards. Strike, or rather tighten, firmly at any unusual behaviour of the float.

There are times in the autumn and winter when grayling will take a fly. As the weather gets colder they will be more likely to take a wet fly or nymph but there are sudden mild days when they will be quite happy to go for a dry fly. The most widely used method for autumn and winter on the Wye is undoubtedly trotting a bait and all that has already been said about summer fishing applies to winter fishing for grayling, except that you stand a better chance in the quieter deeper stretches when the weather and water get really cold.

It is often said that grayling are not deterred by really cold weather and it is quite true to say that, as with salmon fishing, the winter cold affects the fisherman much more than it does the fish. As long as you are really warmly dressed there is always a chance of good fishing with winter grayling.

Another advantage of autumn and winter fishing is that the weed menace, which can be a real problem in the summer, will have passed. In summer there may be periods when the float is constantly being fouled or the line dragged by fragments of weed. In the winter you have no such problems and the float can run free and true. The number of winter grayling caught on the Wye proves how popular they are with coarse fishermen and the trout licence allows the game fisherman to join in the fun.

13
Perch

There are many fine perch in the Wye but the numbers do not compare with the vast populations of chub and dace. It comes as almost a relief to be able to say that they are much more locally distributed and, in addition, even when you have found a perch area, the fish may not be so easy to pinpoint as might be imagined.

It is true that perch are shoal fish and when you catch one you should catch more. However, you first have to find the shoal and I think it must be admitted that this often happens by accident rather than design. Almost every good medium-depth stream on the Wye will have a resident head of chub and dace but not so with the perch. The shoal moves around looking for a plentiful supply of easily obtained food and it would be unwise to think that because you had caught perch in a particular place on one day you would necessarily catch them there on your next outing.

As to perch areas, Hay must be one of the best with fish of 3lb and upwards being caught from time to time. A 3¾-pounder came from there in 1978 and this sort of thing happens most years. Other good places are Moccas, Whitney and Bredwardine and some nice fish of 2lb or more come from as far upstream as Builth. Kington, on the Lugg, can be another useful area. Over the years the records indicate that the best chances of catching big perch are to be had in the middle and upper reaches of the river.

Likely places in perch areas for putting you in the vicinity of the fish are where there is a good depth of water immediately under the bank. The bends and twists in the river generally determine where the main force of the current strikes the banks and where there are trees or bushes at the water's edge the roots will frequently hold the bank together while allowing the water to erode around them. This can provide good conditions for contacting perch but the formula doesn't always work and sometimes the reverse may help. If the bank is soft and the current is directed towards it the result may be that the bank gets gradually washed away. But if the angle of the river is just right and the bank soft on the side opposite the main current the soil can be sucked away from the soft bank leaving it with a good depth of water and possibly undercut. As in all fishing matters there is no simple answer to a problem like this but it is useful to have a few clues as to what to look for. Having said that you might find that the next time you contact perch the shoal is yards from the bank in medium-depth, apparently open, water. They prefer a gravel or clay bottom to fine silty mud. Another point is that as perch get bigger the size of the shoal gets smaller until the really large ones may be hunting in twos or threes, all about the same size.

When after perch it is essential to remember that even when you have been fortunate enough to find the shoal you can completely ruin your chances of success by not being quiet and careful in your movements. Big perch like to get tight in amongst bankside roots and other cover where they can lie in wait for their prey and it is by no means impossible that you could be standing almost on top of them. If you still insist on dropping your kit on the ground, walking heavily around and talking loudly as your ten-foot shadow falls on the water, your chances of catching those perch are going to be completely ruined. It is so easy to think that as water is not our natural element there is no need to worry much how we approach its natural inhabitants. Don't ever get caught in this way whether fishing for perch or anything else. Water is a fine conductor of sound and other vibrations and fish interpret them accordingly.

For general perch fishing the ideal rod is about 10ft long with a powerful through action as opposed to a tip action. The power will be needed to hold a strong fish if it makes a bolt for cover on being hooked. If allowed much leeway because of a weak rod or a less than determined response from the angler that perch is as good as lost. For this reason I should not use less than a 6lb line when after big perch, matched to a good quality hook, size 6 to 8. For close-in fishing or trotting, my own favourite reel is still a centrepin. However, a fixed-spool reel is perfectly satisfactory

A superb catch of plump perch from the river near Whitney

and it has obvious advantages if you are fishing some distance out in the stream.

Worms, maggots and small live or dead fish are all good baits. Lobworms are gladly accepted by perch and they are a bait which requires a minimum amount of time to mount or replace.

I have already mentioned that perch are frequently found in places where there are lots of snags for the hook, such as roots or sunken branches, but if you want to catch perch these are the places you must be prepared to fish. You often have to get the bait right in amongst the obstructions if you are going to tempt the bigger, more solitary fish and it is not much good just trotting a bait past the area. This inevitably means that you are going to get caught up and will lose hooks and for this reason it is prudent to use a slightly lighter hook length. If you do find yourself stuck fast and a break has to be made you do at least escape with a minimum of damage. When you do become caught up do everything possible to get clear with as little disturbance as possible otherwise you might as well pack up and leave that spot. Fortunately, in spite of all the cutting of bankside trees and bushes that has been done over the years to aid land drainage, nature has quietly gone to work again to replace the cover that fish need.

Float fishing for perch, or any other perch fishing, is not a sedentary occupation and the secret is frequent movement. You have to be prepared to change position and cover quite a lot of ground if you are after the big specimens. You can certainly have some time-consuming sport if you get stuck into a shoal of medium-sized perch and this can be good fun. But if it is the big perch you are after it is very unlikely that you will catch more than two or three in any one place. You should consider youself lucky if this does happen to you.

During the summer perch are usually found off the bottom and the shoal will converge on minnows or other prey causing them to flee in all directions and making quite a disturbance on the surface of the water. Under these conditions a freelined lobworm, or as large a worm as you have, can be deadly. As long as there is enough weight in the bait for casting do not add any lead at all, so the bigger the worm the better. You will soon learn to judge the speed at which the bait sinks and this will give

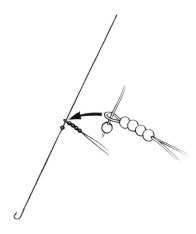

A simple, but effective, link-leger can be made by pinching several large shot on to a loop of nylon line. The main line is threaded through and the link leger is prevented from sliding down on to the baited hook by pinching a shot on the main line at the required distance from the hook

you a reasonable idea of the depth at which fish are feeding when they take the bait. This can be a useful pointer should you decide to change over to using a float for trotting maggots or worms.

For float fishing start at about middle water and gradually lower the bait towards the bottom before deciding that the perch are not present. The float will probably need to be fairly heavy to carry the shot needed to get the bait down quickly to a fishing depth, especially if there is a good current. The first indication that a perch is at the bait is often a dithering of the float. Perch will take a bait in their mouths gently and eject it, doing this several times before really taking it properly. Therefore the hooking of perch requires a certain amount of care, and it is no good striking at the first movement of the float. In fact striking is not the right word: tightening is much better. The perch has a mouth which can expand considerably to accommodate its prey but that mouth is quite tender and a fierce strike will tear it. Maggots can be fished in a similar manner, when they are allowed, but a smaller hook will be needed. If the fish are close in to the bank a couple of dust shot will be all that is needed to get the maggots sinking gently through the shoal and fishing can be fast and furious.

Big perch fishing is a much more leisurely business. Success comes less frequently than with small perch but when it does come the prize is so much better. Catching the big perch is, in some ways, rather like tempting pike when they are not really hungry. You have to go after them and present the bait right under their noses. Because of the possible problems of getting the bait to them the approach has to be determined and you have to vary the method according to the place being fished.

Fortunately the Wye is, in many places, still a fairly leisurely river for the fisherman so there is plenty of room and plenty of quiet places for the roving angler.

While perch will take at any time it is probably when the leaves begin to fall that perch fishing really comes into its own. At this time chub and dace may not be quite so forthcoming but, if you can find him, the perch will not let you down.

For those big perch fish the lob slowly and near the bottom and get it right in amongst the snags. If you feel that a spot out in the stream could be good, try legering a lob with a link leger. Make a loop of monofilament over the line and secure it with enough shot to hold bottom. Place a stop shot about 12in from the bait to prevent the loop moving down to the lob. In really cold conditions bring the stop shot nearer the bait, down to about 8in.

Apart from float fishing or legering, live or dead baiting can be very good for perch. Although you use a float for livebaiting the method seems to be a completely different one from float fishing with worm or maggot. You will need a float which is capable of supporting the bait, probably a minnow, together with the shot necessary to hold the bait down in the water. The bait is hooked through the upper lip and allowed to search the water for you. Alternatively you can use a livebait, hooked in the same way, with a paternoster. The bait is fished from about 10in of monofilament, about 1ft from the bottom, with the bait length attached to the eye of a swivel. I personally prefer deadbaits. These are threaded with a baiting needle through the mouth and out at the vent. A single hook, about 6 or 8, is attached and pulled into the corner of the mouth, or a small treble can be used. In a gentle current it may be possible to freeline the bait but if there is a good current you either have to run a short piece of fine lead piping—the old covering of electric light cable is excellent—along the line and into the mouth or you have to use a leger. In the latter case place a stop shot only about 6in from the bait.

For fairly deep water close to the bank try a minnow. These can be freshly caught or salted, in which state they will last for months. Again, hook the bait through the upper lip and put on a swan shot, about 3in from the bait. Drop the minnow gently over the edge and allow it to flutter freely down into the water. A fixed-spool reel is good for this because you just have to open the bale arm and let the bait draw off the line. If nothing happens on the way down reel the bait back up in a slow erratic manner, varying the speed of wind and moving the rod a little from side to side. For covering larger areas with a deadbait the sink and draw method is good. Once again, use a baiting needle to pass the line through the bait from the mouth and out of the body just before the tail. Add a suitable treble hook at the tail and draw the hook in gently to hold the bait. Weight can be added at the head either by inserting a small length of lead cable cover or a barrel lead into the mouth. Alternatively, a small drilled bullet can be put on the line and held tight against the head of the bait with a stop shot.

In the colder heavier water of winter many perch will be taken by baits on or very near the bottom and moving slowly if at all. In mild weather a rolling leger can be good, held on the bottom for a while then lifted with the rod point for the current to take it a little way downstream.

You can spin with a natural bait mounted on a spinning flight and minnows are great for this. Alternatively a wobbler or Mepps is worth a try. These types of artificial baits are much more attractive to perch than the normal straightforward devon which I would not use out of choice.

Reports in recent years indicate that perch are on the increase in the Wye. While angling successes may not come as regularly as with chub and dace the very elusiveness of perch makes them a worthy quarry.

14
Pike

The Wye could well be the finest pike river in the country and the potential is still largely untapped. Plenty of big pike are caught every year and this is in spite of the fact that, generally speaking, they are not pursued with the blend of skill, knowledge and determination which are necessary for the capture of really big fish.

Finding pike on the Wye is fairly easy and they can be caught anywhere from about Rhayader downstream. In the upper reaches of the river the fish tend to be smaller. The big ones begin occurring round about Glasbury and there is a much better chance of connecting with one of them from here down into the middle reaches, through Hereford and Ross. The lower waters on down through Monmouth also hold large pike. So widely spread are they that it is quite fascinating to look through the records of some of the fish caught. How about this for a choice, by no means exhaustive: Hay area—23 and 25lb; again, fish of 18, 20 and 29lb at Moccas; 283 pike actually reported in the Hay district in 1977; then downstream to Hereford and fish of 22 and 33½lb, followed by a 30-pounder at Sellack; 31½lb at Clyro; 22, 24 and 26¾lb at Ross; 90lb of pike caught by two anglers fishing the weir pool at Hampton Court on the Lugg, and a 32-pounder caught in the Monnow in 1959. All these fish, only a sample of the specimens yielded by the Wye, are topped by that magnificent 37lb fish caught on the Moor water at Hay by Major Booth in 1910 when spinning for salmon with a wagtail bait. It is obvious, then, that good pike can be caught in most areas of the river but they still have to be sought out and vigorously pursued if really good results are to be achieved.

If you intend to use bait fishing and spinning for pike you will need two rods. A 9ft 6in hollow glass rod is the normal one for spinning an artificial bait but it will be too supple for handling much larger weights. The total weight of a live- or deadbait and tackle may vary between 3 and 8oz and the rod will have to be strong enough to handle this kind of load. In addition, a somewhat longer rod is useful for bait fishing and the extra 6in of a 10ft rod can help enormously, giving better bait control. This is especially important when we remember that most Wye pike fishing is done from the bank. I should not hesitate to use a 15 or 16lb line with Alasticum wire for the trace of about the same strength. As long as the technique of presenting the bait is sound pike will not be put off by the stout tackle. They are certainly not hook-shy.

It is well known that pike are partial to dace and roach, both shoaling fish, so it is not unreasonable to expect to find good pike in areas where these fish abound. Much smaller, but very acceptable to pike, are gudgeon. Dace abound through most of the Wye system but roach, although there are plenty of them and their numbers are increasing, tend to be more localised. The Hay to Hereford area is good and Ross produces some nice roach. The Hay area and lower Lugg are well endowed with gudgeon.

Apart from personal convenience the angler's favourite pike-fishing method is likely to decide which area of the Wye he chooses for his sport. If he prefers to live- or deadbait with roach it is obviously less time-consuming and more productive to concentrate on those areas where the roach population is high. This is not so important for the angler who prefers dace as bait and the choice is wide open if you preserve baits for future use when you catch a lot at one time. They can be placed in a suitable container between layers of salt, where they will keep for months. Salted baits go hard and brittle but a few minutes' soaking in water will soon return them to quite reasonable condition. Although not as good as fresh baits preserved ones can be invaluable at a time when bait cannot be caught and an angler who uses artificial baits is free to roam as he pleases. However, a natural bait of 6in or even more stands the best chance of taking really big pike. Having said that I should repeat that the record Wye pike was caught on a wagtail minnow being spun for salmon.

For best results on a river like the Wye we need to find the spots which give the pike the advantages it needs if it is to survive. These are mainly suitable resting places, often with some form of cover, near to but frequently not amongst, a good supply of food fish. The pike usually lies in somewhat deeper water than that loved by the summer dace and it is on the edges of these streams, near a sunken tree or heavy weed-bed that you will find him. Fortunately he also lies on a clean bottom at times and goes unnoticed by his prey. The confluence of a tributary or stream with the main river is another likely place. There may be a scouring effect where the tributary comes into the river and the creation of quiet backwaters and side currents can be ideal places for the pike to lie up while waiting for the pangs of real hunger before moving out to feed in earnest again.

It is no problem attracting a pike when it is really hungry but as this may be on one day in three, depending on how big his last meal was, the task of catching a really big one begins to look a little more difficult. If we remember also that a big pike will, if it can, capture a sufficiently large meal at one attack to assuage its hunger it becomes obvious that pike are actively searching for food for a comparatively short part of their lives.

This is not to say that they will not take a bait at other times but it does mean that we have to pay particular attention to presenting it in the right place and in the right way if we are to stand any reasonable chance of success. In addition the taking of the bait at such times is likely to be less positive than when the fish really needs food. These are the times when a pike may take a long time to swallow the bait, simply resting near the bottom and holding the bait across the middle. It may even eject it completely if it feels a sudden pull on the line or unusual resistance through the bait.

I have come across several examples of this when fishing myself. In one case the fish had been spotted in about 4ft of clear, very slow, water quite close to my own bank. I moved quietly upstream of it and then, slowly and gently, lowered an unweighted dace towards the spot. The bait was apparently taken but the pike did not move and having lost several pike recently when striking I was curious to see what was happening this time. I put the rod carefully down, slipped the check off the reel, and went carefully downstream until I was once again opposite the spot where I knew the fish should be. He was there alright, resting on the bottom with the dace across his jaws making absolutely no effort to swallow it. I watched that fish for several minutes but there was no sign of any movement. Eventually, I went back upstream, picked up the rod gently and reeled quietly in a little then really leaned back into the rod. There was a brief flurry and the bait came back with a few teeth marks on it but otherwise untouched.

Pike in comparatively good condition are taken in the Wye throughout the summer because they obtain their food easily by attacking from ambush in weed or other cover, but they reach tip-top condition later in the year and September to about February is the best time for them.

The pike uses the senses of sight, smell and sound to track down and attack its prey and it seems able to pick up the distress signals from a livebait at some distance. It is obviously attracted by the scent of an oily herring legered for its approval. Its eyes are set well up in the head and it has a wide field of vision both forwards and upwards. In addition it is well camouflaged even when lying on the bottom of the river in a weed-free area. Its good eyesight enables it to identify specifically prey which it has already become aware of through one of its other senses and it can launch itself forward at a very high speed to quickly intercept and catch its prey. It is the element of surprise which makes the pike such a successful hunter and its quarry seems quite unable to realise that an attack may be imminent. Some of the very big loch pike have been caught with salmon inside them and pike will often account for trout. In spite of this it is now realised that quite a large proportion of a pike's food is found by scavenging, and dead fish are simply picked up off the bottom of the river.

It is impossible to know accurately when pike will be feeding but there are certain pointers which should be taken into consideration. Prospects are generally good when the temperaure of the air is higher than that of the water and bad when the water temperature is higher than that of the air. Even when it is really cold in winter a rising air temperature either on one day or, preferably, over a few days will bring pike on the feed. Once the air temperature is up a period of settled weather should be good for sport. For after a particularly cold snap a steady rise of just a few degrees in the air temperature can work wonders for pike fishing. A dull windy day can be good too because the disturbance of the surface of the water and the lack of hard detail in the soft light tend to encourage pike to feed in a more definite manner. During the winter the warmest time, or rather the least cold, is often around midday.

I had a fine and quite unexpected evening of pike fishing late one September. I had been spinning for salmon all day and apart from one small fish in the morning had seen nothing else. About 6 o'clock in the evening a tinge of colour began to come into the river from heavy rain further upstream and the level started to rise. It was an incredible evening and one that I will never forget. At the first signs of fresh water the salmon packed their bags and were off upstream. It was probably the hint of fresh water which had made them restless and uncooperative during the day, but as numerous salmon rose on their way through the beat other fish responded to the fresh water in a different way. Chub and dace began rising madly everywhere and a few big trout joined in. Then, in the shallows at the water's edge and in the run on the far side pike began to feed. There were flurries and splashes everywhere as the pike hunted and I knew I must be on to a good thing.

I quickly changed the small minnow I was using for a homemade wobbler and cast across the stream. The bait was snatched immediately and I promptly hooked a pike only to lose it straight away as its teeth cut the line. I also lost a prized wobbler which had caught me a lot of salmon. Fortunately I had my fishing box with me on the bank and I quickly put on about 10in of Alasticum wire and another wobbler, about 3in long and coloured green and yellow. Everywhere I cast pike seemed to be queuing up for the privilege of taking the bait and by the time I stopped fishing I had caught eight nice pike, the largest weighing just under 18lb. It wasn't an enormous catch but it delighted and interested me. It was made in the space of not much more than an hour on a water which is fished regularly and hard for salmon with all sorts of baits normally acceptable to pike as well. I had no idea that there were still so many pike in the stretch and although odd ones were caught I had never experienced anything like this before. It just shows how easy it is for even proficient anglers to be mistaken concerning the number of pike in any particular water.

It is not generally appreciated that if a pike is not really hungry it may be quite difficult to get it to take a bait and, when it does, the take can be tentative and indefinite. When they are hungry pike will eat almost anything but at other times they have to be very carefully tempted to take.

As far as spinning is concerned pike prefer a bait which flutters and vibrates rather than a straight spinning minnow. I don't think there is any doubt about this although pike are certainly caught on minnows. Something like a large Mepps, a good jointed plug or a Colorado spoon are excellent and it appears quite likely that the vigorous action of these baits may have more to do with their attractiveness than the need for them to be any particular colour.

When spinning for pike, spin slowly and deeply, exactly the same as you would for spring salmon, and follow the undulations of the bottom whenever possible. A big Mepps will spin with a minimum of movement and current so it is possible to fish it quite slowly. In some cases lead may have to be added but keep it to a minimum. Because of the need to fish a bait deep in the water spinning can be troublesome in summer because of the presence of heavy weed growth in many places. Under these conditions a wobbler or River Runt plug offers the best bet. The plug floats until drawn quickly through the water when the fin makes it dive. Plugs are excellent for fishing weed-bound areas and breaks in weed-beds. After casting and fishing as much as possible of the clear water stop winding so that the bait comes to the surface. It can then be reeled very gently to draw it over the weed or the rod can be raised fairly high and the bait plucked from the water. Do not use lead when fishing a plug; it is not necessary.

When fishing any of these artificial baits strike immediately a fish is felt and do not expect a tremendous pull every time. Sometimes the take is quite gentle, again just like a salmon, and to delay the strike is to lose the fish. Always use a wire trace for pike. You will certainly land some without wire but you will definitely lose a lot more and probably the best ones.

Experiences with pike are the subject of more fishing stories than any other fish in our rivers and this particular one has always left me with a nagging uncertainty. I had decided to try and catch a very big chub that had taken up lodgings close to a huge sunken tree which had stuck fast on the edge of a slow deep stream. I was freelining a large lobworm quietly down along the trunk of the tree from a seat in one of the branches and as I pulled the worm to the surface it was seized vigorously by a little pike of about 1lb. I brought it to the side and was holding it there waiting to see whether it would eject the worm or whether I would have to get the hook out myself when a huge dark shape rose from below and the small pike was grabbed across the middle by the biggest pike I have ever seen. The fish gently shook the little pike then rolled quietly over and sank back out of sight. I was so astonished that it was a couple of seconds before I lifted the rod to find that the teeth of the monster had sliced through the line and I was dangling the broken end in the water. I swear that pike was well over 30lb and it did me no good at all to know that I may even have had a tangle with a record fish. Two of us tried everything we knew for a fortnight, on and off, to get the pike to come again but we never saw a sign of it afterwards.

I have no idea what the pike population of the Wye is. There have always been masses of them in the river and really big ones too, but it looks as though their numbers are going to increase rapidly. After the drought of the 1976 season very large numbers of tiny pike were reported from many areas and records indicate that a pike explosion took place. Large numbers of small fish are still being caught and it looks as though everything is set for a further build-up in the numbers of these exciting fish.

Natural-bait fishing consists of float fishing, legering or using a paternoster with either live- or deadbaits and the first two methods are most widely used on the Wye. For float fishing with livebait some pike bungs are still used but big balsa floats, with a longer slimmer shape are now more popular. You will probably be fishing in not more than 6 or 7ft of water and the usual method is to fish the bait not more than about 1ft off the bottom. The bait can be held down in the water by a drilled bullet kept at the required depth by a stop shot. Sometimes a pilot float is added to the rig and stopped upline at a distance

Coarse fishing on the Wye at Ross-on-Wye

which exceeds the maximum expected depth of water. It is used either as a second indicator if the main float is drawn below the surface or to help keep the line afloat. I never use one and prefer to grease the line if I particularly want it to keep well afloat when fishing at a distance.

Dace or small roach are the most frequently used livebait. They can be hooked through the upper lip only with about a 2/0 single hook or a snap tackle can be used. Take care in casting, particularly with the more delicately single-hook-mounted baits as they will easily fly off if they are cast too vigorously. Let the bait search the eddies and holes and trot it very slowly down

149

under fairly deep water beneath bankside trees, especially where there is a stream or drain outfall.

If you use large livebaits of 8in or more you will need to be very careful indeed about judging the moment for striking, otherwise you will lose a lot of fish. The bigger baits tend to mask the hooks more and pike often seem able to eject baits which they have been holding, apparently firmly, for some time. Give more time with a single-hook mount than with a multi-hook one. Be prepared to give slack line at first, even with a snap tackle, and this is really important when trying to catch fish which are not hungry. They are then more cautious in their feeding habits. Anything like undue resistance on the line or the sight of the angler may make them drop the bait.

On cold days it can be good to paternoster or leger a livebait and be prepared to wait quite a long time in one spot before deciding that there is nothing there. An occasional slight pull in of the bait can help a pike, which may have been watching the bait for some time, to make up its mind and take it.

Personally I am not fond of livebaiting these days and although I recognise its effectiveness I prefer to use a deadbait. Herring has several excellent attributes. It is soft, so the hooks do not have too much to pull against and they pull out easily from the bait when the strike is made. In addition there is undoubtedly a great attraction for pike in the oily texture of the flesh which leaks a steady trail of oil while it is on the bottom. Also, of course, it is much easier to obtain a supply of fresh herrings than it is to obtain and keep alive a quantity of livebait.

There are numerous variations in the types of snap tackle but the idea is to arrange the hooks so that they hold the bait firmly but do not lever against it and hook inefficiently when the pike takes. I use a snap tackle with two trebles, which is the most usual number these days. One treble is at the end of the wire and the other is kept loose and 'flying' so that it can be adjusted on the wire to take its proper place on the bait. One way to mount the bait is to put two points of the bottom treble through the mouth from below and set the other treble on the side just slightly in front of the dorsal fin. Alternatively, one point of the bottom treble can be pressed into the belly of the bait below the head and the wire wound around the bait near the dorsal fin to set the other hook at the front of that fin. An Arlesey Bomb with a stop shot 6 to 10in from the bait should be adequate, depending on the current. The quieter medium-depth places with a clear bottom are the best for legering a deadbait.

In cold weather you might have to wait quite a long time for a fish to pick up the bait so don't get restless too quickly. You may also find it quite difficult to judge the moment for the strike. If a pike is hungry he may swallow the bait almost as soon as he sees it and picks it up while, on other days, he may pick it up and drop it several times before taking hold of it 'for keeps'. It will be advisable to wait a little while when the bait is moved by a fish to see what happens. If it moves a little distance away and then stops, strike when the line begins to move again. The process may take quite a time especially with a big bait like a herring. On other occasions it may be quite safe to strike with a snap tackle almost as soon as a real movement is seen.

With all pike fishing ensure that the hooks are kept needle sharp and examine them frequently, especially after running a fish. Use a small hone to keep the hooks sharp, working towards the bend from the point. Another important thing which is easily forgotten when pike fishing is the need to move quietly and carefully. In spite of their predatory nature and apparent aggressiveness they can be easily alerted by noise and careless movements.

When striking a pike the best way is to reel up until you can just, but only just, feel the fish, then lean back firmly and hold the rod there for a couple of seconds. This should set the hooks well. A sudden slashing strike can put a severe strain on tackle and may cause a break or badly weaken the line. Don't forget to gag a pike before trying to remove the hooks and use a pair of pliers. You really can get very painful lacerations from a pike's teeth, so be warned. Renew the trace if there is the slightest indication of any kinking or sharp bending of the wire. When gaffing a pike slide the point in gently underneath the chin and lift straight upwards. Do not twist the gaff or drag the fish out of the water.

15
Roach

Roach are found in considerable numbers in many parts of the Wye and its tributaries although you have to look more carefully for them than for chub or dace. Reports from anglers and bailiffs indicate quite clearly that the numbers of roach in the Wye are increasing and this must be good news for all coarse fishermen. The Hereford area is one where an improvement in the roach fishing has been noted and the Hay district has a good head of these fish.

Other places which have reported good roach recently include the Lugg with a 2¼lb fish in 1977 and the Llynfi with a 2lb 2oz specimen. 18lb were caught on Ross Town water and other fine roach have come from the Monnow, the Carrots water and the Arrow. This pretty fish is very adaptable and is found in water conditions which range from fairly shallow to quite deep and swiftly or slowly moving. Its colouring is beautiful—lovely silvery flanks with a bluish-green back and red fins and it is no wonder that the roach is the coarse fisherman's most popular quarry and roach fishing one of the most fascinating forms of coarse fishing.

I suppose the best all-round rod for Wye roach fishing would be a fast-action hollow glass or carbon fibre one of 12 to 13ft. A 12-footer is fine if you are frequently able to get the fish in fairly close but if you often have to get well out from the bank, and the Wye is a wide river, a rod of at least 13ft will be needed. It is surprising how much difference an extra foot or two on a rod can make. Sometimes it can be rather a nuisance if you are fishing in a confined space but in other conditions the longer rod gives better float control and keeps more line off the water. This aids speed of striking and for roach this is a most important point.

Fortunately, apart from some of the heavily fished club waters, there are still plenty of places on the Wye where roach are not hammered and I see no reason to go lower than a 4lb line on most occasions. A size 16 hook should be small enough for any occasion and with the larger baits a size 14 or even a 12 is perfectly acceptable. There are lots of excellent lines on the market these days but I like a soft smooth one, with a dull surface, not one which looks harsh and bright, almost as though it had been varnished. I think this is quite important for roach fishing where the quarry is a naturally shy, retiring fish.

Wye roach are quite happy to accept most of the usual roach baits like maggots, casters, paste or flake, as well as small worms. Maggots must catch more Wye roach than anything else but they are, of course, the most frequently used bait anyway. Remember that, at present, maggots may not be used between the 14 March and the 26 October.

When float fishing for roach, which is the most popular method, try to ensure that the float and shot are kept as light as possible. A certain amount of weight will be needed for casting and this, together with weather and water conditions, will decide what type of float should be used. A well-shotted quill float will provide less resistance to a taking fish than a bulkier one or one which is not shotted enough. Another advantage of having the float shotted correctly is that it will be more sensitive to many types of light bites. These are often scarcely more than a touch and they can easily go unnoticed until you know what to look for.

Because they are shy roach tend to prefer water over about four feet in depth, particularly when conditions are bright and clear. In addition they like a good clean bottom and in the Wye this generally means rock or gravel. You are very unlikely to find them in the Wye where the bottom is muddy.

In the summer long tendrils of water ranunculus frequently divide the current and where this happens and the water begins to open out again is often a good place to find roach. Otherwise slow-to-moderate-paced streams over a good clean bottom are worth investigating. If you are seriously after these summer fish and the conditions are really bad—low clear water and bright hard light—it is best to avoid the hottest hours and concentrate your efforts in the early morning and evening. Roach can be notoriously fickle when the river is bright and still, with nothing moving, but a few hours either way can make all the difference. The addition of a slight breeze on a bright day should be eagerly accepted as the bonus it is. Groundbaiting can be a tricky business, especially in summer, and the consistency needs to be just right. Bread and bran is good and it needs to be mixed so that it goes to the bottom and then sends up a regular stream of particles. This is particularly important in fairly deep water where there is a good current. If the bait breaks up too quickly it will be whipped away before the fish get a chance to inspect it properly. The deeper the water the further upstream you may have to throw the groundbait and don't make the balls too big. Drop them in to the water as quietly as you can. Bombarding roach with great heavy balls of groundbait can put them right off and, where practicable, loosefeeding may be the answer.

If I'm not sure of the depth I prefer to check it by overshotting a float and adjusting until I get it right. This causes less disturbance than using a plummet and, in my opinion, is much better. Finding the shoal is often a trial-and-error business and you may have to move around quite a bit before you strike lucky. Because of their shyness the fish may be well out in the stream but it does not always follow by any means and if there is a suitable swim you can find them in quite close. If disturbed by fishermen, or anyone else making a noise on the bank, the shoal will move away and it becomes more difficult and time-consuming to contact them again. They could also be edgy when you do find them and, therefore, more difficult to catch.

One of the best days I have ever had with Wye roach occurred below Hay. I arrived at the river at about 6.30 on a beautiful still morning on what was obviously going to be a scorching-hot day. I knew a shoal had been about on the previous day but when I began fishing I did not know what had happened to it. I was fishing paste, just a small piece on a 14 hook and after checking the depth began trotting a lovely bankside swim. The water was between five and six feet deep and I could hardly believe my luck or my eyes as the float dipped for an instant almost at once. I missed that fish but was soon well and truly amongst them. It was only after I had caught three or four nice fish of just over a pound that I realised that in my excitement I had not put in any loosefeed. That day it didn't seem to matter but I threw in a

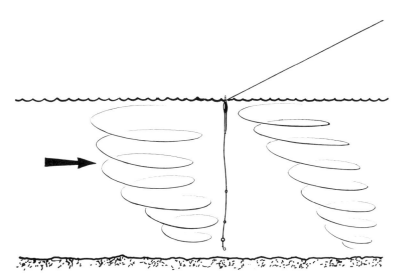

In swims with swirling underwater currents it is often best to put the bulk of the shot near the hook to get the bait down quickly. This can be done either by bunching all the shot near the hook, or by spacing the shot with the largest one nearest the hook, as above

little, just for luck. I had caught fifteen lovely roach when my luck changed. An early-rising holidaymaker was exercising his dog along the bank as I hooked another fish. The next moment a large stick flew over my head into the water closely followed by a black labrador and that was the end of my fishing. I landed my roach but after that everything went dead and I had to pack up that spot. Admittedly the man did not know I was there because I was quietly tucked down under the bank but I have little doubt that he and his dog ruined for me what had every indication of being a record day.

Summer roach in easy water are likely to give a tiny pluck to the float and you must respond instantaneously and crisply otherwise you will be too late. Anything which arouses their suspicion will result in the immediate rejection of the bait. In faster water fish have less time to inspect the bait and the bite is more positive and easier to detect and hook. They will also take more boldly as the river begins to rise and a hint of colour shows.

Incidentally, the surface of the water is by no means always a good guide as to what is happening below. Sometimes lower water moves more slowly or more quickly than the surface and this can play havoc with the presentation of a bait. If the roach

155

are in such a spot you may have to place lead nearer the hook than you would normally do to get it down to where the fish are feeding. In some of these peculiar places the fish can be facing downstream in a reverse current.

Good water conditions for fishing can bring their own problems. Summer float fishing on the Wye can be very good especially, as I have just said, when there is a little rise and some colour. Unfortunately, in the middle and lower reaches, this is just the time when the heavier flow starts to break off fragments of the long river weed and it can be a real nuisance when it keeps wrapping itself around the line or fouling the float. There is not much that can be done about this because a change to legering does not help. However, with the fish less shy and feeding more freely it pays to carry on patiently fishing and removing the weed. Usually the problem vanishes after a day or two, until the next rise in water level.

Some thought will have to be given to the position of the shots on the line and this is partly governed by the weight of the bait. For a heavy bait like worm about 18in from the hook may be right for the last shot, while for buoyant baits like breadcrust or flake the lowest shot should come much nearer the hook, say about 6in. The method will vary, of course, depending on whether you want the bait down to its fishing depth as quickly as possible or whether you want to fish it more on the drop. Earlier on I mentioned that quill floats are good but in deeper, faster places you may need a bodied, Avon-type float to carry the extra shot.

Fishing on the drop can be very good for roach. Arrange the shot with the heaviest not far below the float and then in diminishing size with an unweighted tail of 2ft or more. With this rig the float will cock soon after hitting the water and will settle further as the lower shot takes effect. The trail will sink fairly slowly, depending on the weight of the bait and you need to watch very carefully for the indication of a bite. Depending on what position the bait is in and how the fish take it the float should dip or rise, dither or slow down. You might even feel or see nothing and if the bait is obviously being sampled it is a good idea to shorten the fishing depth or the trail, or both.

Although I said earlier that summer roach do not like hot

An angler fishing the Whitney Court water in May (*John Tarlton*)

conditions, I should, perhaps, mention that a lot of roach are caught on the Wye in the summer but many of them are caught on the more overcast days. On a hot afternoon you are much more likely to catch small roach rather than the fine specimens the Wye can produce.

If you have to trot the bait a long distance striking can be a problem. Quite apart from becoming less efficient as the distance increases, it also puts an increasing strain on the line and breaks can result. This is particularly true if the float is fastened top and bottom but the situation can be eased somewhat by fastening the float only at the bottom. Place a small shot about 4in either side of the bottom ring so that the strike does not have to saw the float through the water quite so much.

There are quite a few places on the Wye, particularly on the upper river and between Ross and Monmouth, where the valley seems to act like a funnel to the wind and conditions can get very gusty. If the wind is downstream try using one of the Ducker-type floats. These are shotted to get the body well down in the water so that only the antenna is showing. The float is attached by the bottom ring only and it is usual to put a small shot about 12in above the float to sink the line and steady things up a little. I think there is some truth in the belief that larger baits tend to take larger roach. Although shy, smaller roach are not as wary as the big ones and the little fish often beat the big ones to the smaller baits and take them before the old stagers have made up their minds.

Legering can be a good roach method although it is not used very much on the Wye. It is used more, and tends to be more effective, in autumn and winter. At this time of year roach shoals tighten up and tend to grow larger as winter conditions approach. One of the best baits must be a lob-tail but redworm, maggots, casters and bread can all be good. A 4lb line should be alright.

You are now likely to find the fish in deeper easier water than they kept to in summer but they still like that clean river bed. Roach will feed at any time in winter but it is well known that they are susceptible to a sudden drop in temperature. When this happens they go right off the feed but if the temperature stays down they start taking again in a few days. Alternatively, if the temperature suddenly goes back up they begin feeding again quite quickly.

Groundbaiting in winter should be done in less quantities than in summer and, again, with just a little of the hook bait mixed in as a special inducement. You may still have to move from one place to another until you find the fish. Either a pierced bullet or a swan-shot link in the quieter places are excellent methods but in all cases use only a minimum of lead. It is best to hold the rod in the one hand, holding the line with the other rather than using a rest. This is particularly important when the bites are quick and shy. You have to strike at the first fleeting indication and it may be gone almost before the eyes pick it up. Holding the line greatly increases your sensitivity and, hence, your speed of reaction.

For float fishing in winter the bait should move as slowly as possible and on or very near the bottom. You may have to use a shot or two quite low down to ensure that the bait fishes close to the bottom with as little unnecessary movement as possible. You have to balance the advantages of shot low down with the disadvantages of fish which happen to be particularly shy.

I remember seeing a really nice bag of roach taken from the Town water at Ross. The fisherman had taken a few good fish the day before while legering but this day he was using float gear again. He was convinced that the fish were still there and the water conditions and temperature were the same. He fished for half an hour without success and when I came back to him he was just changing the shot pattern to one similar to the one I have just mentioned. On this occasion he had a No 8 shot within about four inches of the bait which was two maggots. In went the float and within fifteen yards the float bobbed and he was into a nice roach. He was fishing a medium-current stream about eight feet deep and it seemed pretty obvious that the one extra shot was getting the bait down and steadying it for the rather lethargic fish to have a go. It's amazing how delicate the adjustments have to be sometimes yet they make all the difference between success and failure.

16
Shad

This mysterious and exciting fish enters the Wye in considerable numbers, usually towards the end of April. Very few rivers in the British Isles see these fish at all but there are big runs in the Wye and Severn. A good place to see them when they are running is at the rapids at Symonds Yat. They keep in close to the bank in the quieter water and you can see them going through, often in little groups of about six. They have a unique, vigorous tail action as they push upstream against the current. They are caught from the bank with the big cleaching net and have been sold under the all-embracing term of rock salmon.

Both Allis and Twaite shad used to be found in the Wye in very large numbers which were sufficient to make commercial fishing both possible and profitable. In more recent years the number of Allis has diminished remarkably and very few are seen each year. The Twaite run is reduced too but not nearly so drastically as the Allis and plenty can still be seen every year.

The Allis is by far the larger of the two, reaching a weight of about 6lb. It is said to enter the Wye a little earlier than the Twaite. Apart from the difference in size (the Twaite are usually a little under 1lb) it is not always easy to positively identify which fish has been caught. The dark spots on the sides are not an infallible guide and the only precise method is to examine the number of gill rakers as there are more in the Allis than the Twaite.

Shad like the temperature of the river water to be higher than that of the sea and they will not normally venture into fresh water until this is the case. Once in the river they immediately begin their vigorous and determined passage upstream to suitable spawning places. Despite the large numbers of shad which have come into the river for a great many years there is little precisely recorded information about their activities in the river and what happens to the fry when they are hatched. Even less is known about what happens to the spawned fish and fry when they leave the estuary.

The male is slightly smaller than the female, returning to the river to spawn after three years, while the female returns after four years. This has been estasblished from scale reading. It has also been discovered that it is not unusual for shad to return two or three times to spawn so that the mortality rate after spawning does not appear to be very high. The fry are larger than would be expected from fish the size of Twaite and small shad have been discovered throughout most of the river. The adult fish certainly penetrate the river as far as Builth. It is believed that when they leave the estuary shad make for the Mediterranean area but this has not yet been conclusively proved. Fish are being tagged in the Wye in an attempt to obtain more precise information about their movements.

While this is very important work and of long-term value to all fishermen, there is nothing mysterious about the behaviour of the fish while in the river, at least not from the angler's point of view. A shoal of shad will quickly make its presence known and they are very exciting to watch as they tear about on the gravelly shallows where they spawn. At such times they virtually ignore the fisherman and while wading in the Wye I have had Twaite boil all around me and actually pass between my legs. Sometimes they make a whirring noise as they skim across the surface of the water and once they are in the river they can nearly always be caught where they are visible. They can also be caught in medium-paced streams of moderate depth, up to about 6 or 8ft where they cannot be seen so easily.

Wet-fly tackle is a splendid way of catching shad and an exciting one. If he is wading, the angler can go to the fish and make contact much more frequently than if he has to wait on the bank for a shoal to come within reach. Shad will take a considerable variety of baits and lures and small fly spoons and Mepps are favourites. Sea-trout and even salmon flies can be taken quite viciously when the fish are in the mood and that seems to be most of the time. The take is normally sharp and a prompt response is needed to set the hook. Cast across the current and move the bait or fly fairly quickly, especially as the

A family outing on the rapids at Symonds Yat (*John Tarlton*)

water warms up. This works best on the shallows but in the streams it often pays to let the fly or bait simply hang in the current in the path of the shoal.

Until you have held a Twaite in your hand it is almost impossible to understand just how muscular and steely they are and what great fighters they can be. They are said to be good to eat provided they are caught fairly soon after entering the river but I must admit that I have never put it to the test. Naturally, their condition deteriorates during their stay in fresh water and as spawning takes place.

If you are not kitted out for wading and do not own fly-fishing tackle you can still have a lot of fun with shad by using a light spinning rod and the small Mepps from the bank. When shad are about they invariably give away their presence by hurtling around the shallows, particularly towards evening when their activity increases. Again concentrate on the shallows and streams with plenty of movement, which are good places for spinning. Shad are sometimes caught on other baits, for example worms, and they provide some good fun when this happens. However, it is the exception rather than the rule. They prefer an interesting, moving lure on most occasions.

If you have not come across shad so far keep an eye open during future visits to the river in May or June for the tell-tale swirls and splashes which indicate that Twaite are about.

17
Other Fish

Bleak were first reported in the Wye in 1973 when three were positively identified in the Hereford area. Not native to the river it appears that their introduction was the result of anglers emptying bait cans at the end of a day's pike fishing. Since they were first reported bleak have been caught at Builth, Hay and Ross and there are now quite a number in the Hereford district. This little shoal-fish feeds at or near the surface and if you want to fish for it you will need to use very light float tackle and a 16 to 18 hook. Maggots are freely accepted as are scraps of worm or tiny pieces of paste or flake. Freelining with any of these baits is also good. Bleak are useful as live- or deadbait, especially for pike.

Another small fish found in the Wye, and this time in large numbers, is the gudgeon. In the summer they love shallow streams with a modest current over clean gravel. Again, widely distributed gudgeon are caught by the thousand in such diverse areas as the lower Lugg, the Monnow, Hay and the lower Arrow. Gudgeon are active feeders and are easily caught on a little redworm, maggots or bread fragment. Anglers out fishing especially for gudgeon like to stir up the bottom of the river at the head of a good stream and possibly add fine groundbait. You can use light float tackle or a clear line with just a couple of small shot. In either case keep the bait touching the bottom as it moves along by placing the shot low down near the hook. A 14 or 16 hook should do fine. When gudgeon fishing on the Wye you will be wise to remember that the method of fishing could easily attract larger fish so don't go below a 2lb line, just in case. Gudgeon are not tackle-shy.

How barbel found their way into the Wye will never be known but odd ones have been caught below Ross and at Erwood. It is too early at this stage to know how they will acclimatise to the Wye but there are plenty of places which seem to be tailor-made for them. Only time will decide whether they flourish in the river or not and what effect their coming will have on the resident fish population. At present there are so few of them that they are caught by accident rather than design and barbel fishing is not a sport to be recommended. However, if you do catch one it is likely to be a very exciting experience.

Odd tench and carp are reported in the Wye itself with tench turning up every so often on the Belmont water at Hereford. Carp are occasionally caught at Ross but more regularly in the Monnow.

The other interesting fish found in the Wye is the lamprey. Brook lampreys are widely distributed from the Irfon down to the middle Monnow. River lampreys are often seen in the Lugg and Monnow and the really big sea lampreys come into the Wye in about May, at the same time as the shad, and get as far upstream as Glasbury and Builth where they can be seen spawning around July. These lampreys may be 30in or so in length.

This chapter on unusual fish would not be complete without mentioning James Postans and the year 1846. In June of that year Postans was fishing in the Wye at the weir, five miles above the city of Hereford, when he saw a huge fish basking quietly in the water. He went after it with a knife and his bare hands and this is how the *Hereford Times* of 3 June 1846 vividly described the incident:

> With panting anxiety and some little trepidation, he watched the proceedings of the huge creature, and pursued it with a determination to become its victor. He struck it with his rod, which, as may be supposed, produced little effect, and equally unsuccessful was the effort to seize it by a kind of sail which was elevated above the water. At last, after a chase and struggle of half an hour, Postans inflicted in succession two deep wounds with a pocket knife which he carried with him but still the creature evinced no disposition to give in. During the struggle which took place in the ford, which was about knee deep, sometimes the man was uppermost and sometimes the fish. The biped and inveterate foe, however, though no little astonished and somewhat daunted, inserted his hand into one of the gashes towards the tail, from which the crimson tide

flowed copiously, and was at last enabled to land his prize, which did not finally give up the ghost till eleven o'clock at night. It proved to be a Royal Sturgeon of the extraordinary length of eight feet six inches, girth three feet, and weight one hundred and eighty two pounds . . .

The fish was brought to this city by Postans on Monday last, and was at first exhibited at Mrs. White's, Widemarsh street, at one penny each but, it being holiday time, the crowds of visitors were so numerous that it was found necessary to change the place of exhibition to the large dining room of the Black Swan Hotel.

Another sturgeon of 131lb was taken in a net as far upstream as Glasbury fourteen years previously. There are no modern records of sturgeon in the Wye but we live in hope.

.

PART 3
WHERE TO FISH

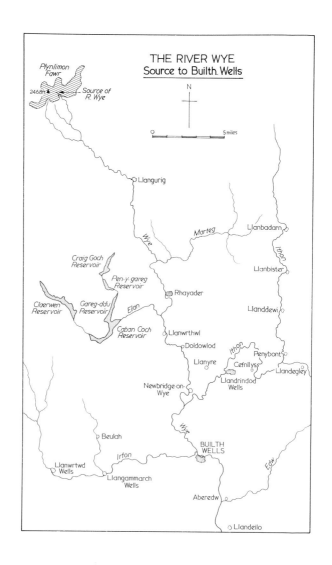

THE RIVER WYE
Source to Builth. Wells

N

5 miles

Plynlimon
Fawr

2468ft — Source of
R. Wye

Llangurig

Wye

Marteg   Llanbadarn

Craig Goch
Reservoir   Ithon

Pen-y-gareg   Llanbister
Reservoir

Claerwen   Gareg-ddu   Elan   Rhayader
Reservoir   Reservoir

Caban Coch   Llanddewi
Reservoir   Llanwrthwl

Doldowlod

Ithon   Penybont
Llanyre

Cefnllys   Llandegley
Llandrindod
Wells
Newbridge-on-
Wye

Wye

Beulah   BUILTH
WELLS
Irfon
Llanwrtwd   Edw
Wells
Llangammarch
Wells

Aberedw

Llandeilo

18

Salmon and Trout

Source to Builth Wells *(See map on page 168)*

The Wye almost falls off Plynlimon, passes under the A44 and is joined at Pont Rhyd-Galed by the equally fast and boulder-strewn Tarenig which, in places, is bigger than the Wye. The river then runs south-east to Llangurig where the course is through hills and fairly straight. At Llangurig the Wye turns almost south and the fall, although still fast, is nowhere near as steep as it is further upstream. The river is less rocky here and keeps quite close to the A470 and about two miles above Rhayader it is joined by the Marteg. Here the Wye makes a tight curve before continuing its south-easterly course to Rhayader. About two miles below Rhayader the Elan comes in on the right bank and the Wye runs close to the Builth road. Below the confluence of the Elan and Wye is Llanwrthwl and further down, on the other bank, Doldowlod. The river then runs south-east to Newbridge and below Newbridge the Ithon enters the Wye from the left bank. The Wye then curves slightly before continuing on its south-easterly course, picking up the Irfon on the right bank at Builth Wells.

In the upper reaches salmon fishing is a late season occupation. The comparative scarcity of salmon in the area for most of the year is indicated by the fact that above Llanwrthwl Bridge, between Newbridge and Rhayader, the season was extended by almost a full month to 25 October, but it is now 17 October throughout the river. Trout are smaller in the upper waters too and the size limit is 7in from the tip of the snout to the fork of the tail. Below Llanwrthwl Bridge the size limit is 8in. Nevertheless the countryside is beautiful and the fishing much cheaper than can be expected further down river.

169

The Hendre water on the Wye comprises 1 mile of trout and salmon fishing adjacent to the A44 about 4 miles out of Llangurig towards Rhayader. Fly and spinning only for trout and the bag limit is 6 fish. Tickets from Mr J. Cameron, Plynlimon Cafe, Llangurig, Powys.

Clockfaen Estate water 8½ miles long and adjacent to the A44 Rhayader to Aberystwyth road. Fly only for trout and there is a bag limit of 6 fish. Access is from gates on the road leading to the river and these must be kept closed. Boundaries are marked by bankside notices. Both of these fisheries are end-of-season waters as far as salmon are concerned.

R. Marteg The Rhayader AA has fishing here and tickets are available from Mrs Powell, Garth House, Rhayader, or R. Davies (Chemist) Rhayader. Some salmon fishing, generally towards the end of the season. Fly, worm and spinning are allowed for trout and the bag limit is 12 fish.

Rhayader The Rhayader AA has fishing on the Wye. Both banks from Duffryn Farm are fishable, about 1 mile below Rhayader to Derw Farm and about ½ mile upstream of Rhayader Bridge. Only local members are allowed to fish for salmon after 30 September. The water is stocked annually with 1,000 8in brown trout and the bag limit is 6 fish.

The Elan Valley Hotel, Elan Village, Nr Rhayader, Powys, has 2½ miles of both banks of the Marteg from its confluence with the Wye to St Harmon. There is also a 4 mile stretch of the Wye on both banks, 3 miles of water above Rhayader and 1 mile below. Day or week tickets available. Glanrhydwen Guest House, Elan Village, Nr Rhayader, has 200yd of the left bank of the Elan which is free to residents.

Doldowlod The Birmingham AA has two lengths of the left bank of the Wye. One extends upstream from the Vulcan Arms for ¼ mile. The other begins at the disused railway bridge and extends downstream for ½ mile. There is a small section of 300yd on the right bank. Trout and salmon are caught here and during the trout season fly only is allowed. To get to the fishing, take the A44 to Rhayader at Cross Gates for 7 miles. Turn left at the Doldowlod sign and the Vulcan Arms is about 3 miles down the road. This is not really an early salmon fishery.

The Vulcan Motel can supply day tickets for 1 mile on the

right bank of the Wye between the site of the railway bridge near Glanryd-grech farm and the boundary of the Doldowlod Estate at Doldowlod old station.

Doldowlod Hall Estate has about 4 miles of water on the Wye and information can be obtained from Mr G. Phillips, Laundry Cottage, Doldowlod, Llandrindod Wells. Spinning and fly only for salmon and fly only for trout. There is no bag limit for trout and the water is stocked annually. Access is off the A470 Newbridge to Rhayader road.

Glanrhos water about ¾ mile of the Wye is available, tickets from Mrs A. Crosland, Llanwthwl, Llandrindod Wells. Spinning and fly only for salmon and fly only for trout. Minimum size for trout is 10in and the water is stocked annually.

Llanbister The BAA has several stretches on the Ithon which is mostly trout water although there are a few salmon late in the season. There is ¾ mile, mostly both banks, at Llanbister. Access is near where the river comes close to the road.

Penybont The BAA has both banks for a short distance above the road bridge by Rabber Farm and a short distance on the right bank below the road bridge. A further ¾ mile of both banks starts a short distance below the railway bridge and there is also fishing from the road bridge at Penybont ½ mile downstream on the left bank. The Penybont water is for fly only.

Penybont The Severn Arms Hotel has about 3 miles, 1 mile of which is adjacent to the hotel; tickets from Mr K. W. Davies, Severn Arms Hotel, Penybont. Fishing is free to residents and there is a bag limit of 6 fish.

Llanbadarn The BAA has about ¾ mile of both banks and ½ mile on the right bank which starts ¼ mile below Alpine Bridge and extends upstream. Below Llanbadarn Road Bridge there is a further ½ mile on the right bank starting below the road bridge and 700yd of the left bank which starts one meadow below the road bridge. The Llanbadarn water is fly only. Mr Harris, Great Cellws Farm, Llandrindod Wells, can supply tickets for 1 mile of fishing on the left bank of the Ithon downstream from Llanbadarn Bridge. No bag limit.

Llanyre The BAA has about 1 mile on the right bank at Lower Dol-Llwynhir Farm, near Llandrindod Wells.

Llanddewi The Severn Arms Hotel, Penybont, has 1½ miles on

171

the Ithon, mostly both banks, between Llanddewi village and Rabber Bridge and also 1½ miles on both banks from Penybont Bridge to Brynthomas Bridge. There is a further mile, one section of which is the left bank but mostly both banks, between Llanbister and Llanddewi village. The Walsh Arms has 1 mile downstream, on both banks of the Ithon, from Llanddewi Bridge. Fishing is free to residents and details can be obtained from Mr C. Daniels. There is no bag limit.

Llandegley Mr D. W. Lewis issues tickets for 1 mile of the left bank downstream of Aber Mithyl Farm, and also for ¼ mile of the right bank below the farm. Fly and worm only and there is no bag limit.

The Brynthomas water has ¾ mile on the left bank downstream of Brynthomas Bridge and ¼ mile on the right bank upstream of the bridge. Tickets are obtainable from Mr Owen, Brynthomas, Penybont, Llandrindod Wells. Fishing is free to residents and there is no bag limit.

Cefnllys The Noyadd Farm has 3 miles: 1 mile of the right bank downstream from Shaky Bridge and 2 miles of left bank upstream from the bridge. Fly and spinner only and tickets are obtainable from Mr W. R. Collard, Noyadd Farm, Cefnllys, Penybont. No bag limit.

Llandrindod Wells The AA has about 5 miles from Llanyre Bridge to Disserth Bridge. Fly and worm allowed with spinning from 1 August. Access is near Llandrindod Wells on the A483 and tickets can be obtained from C. Selwyn & Sons, 4 Park Crescent, Llandrindod Wells. The Metropole and Glen Usk Hotels at Llandrindod Wells can offer fishing to guests on the upper part of the Wye system.

The Dolfawr water Mr R. Tyler of Dolfawr Farm, Newbridge on Wye, can issue tickets for 1½ miles of right bank upstream of Pont ar Ithon Bridge, Newbridge-on-Wye. No bag limit but fish under 8in must be returned.

Llangammarch Wells On the other side of the Wye the Cammarch Hotel has four stretches of fishing, for hotel residents only. On the Dulas, a tributary of the Irfon, there is about ⅔ mile of both banks 1 mile below Pont ar Dulas where it meets the Irfon.

On the Cammarch there are 2½ miles in three stretches upstream of Cammarch Bridge and on the Irfon itself 3½ miles above and below Llangammarch Wells. Most of this fishing is on the left bank. On the Wye there are 2 miles of the left bank where the Irfon comes in at Builth Wells down to the Cnitho brook.

The Cammarch Hotel owns water on three rivers. There is a 1½ mile stretch on the Cammarch from Llangammarch to Blackbridge and a further 1½ miles from Llwncadwgan to Blackbridge. On the Irfon there is a 1¾ mile stretch on the left bank between Garth and Llangammarch and ¾ mile at Llangammarch School. There is also 1 mile above Llanafon weir on the Dulas. Fishing for trout, fly, spinning and worm. Some fly-only water. Tickets from Mr Jones, Cammarch Hotel, Llangammarch Wells, subject to availability.

The Lake Hotel, Llangammarch Wells, has about 4 miles of one bank of the Irfon. Fly only for trout and tickets can be obtained from Mrs J. F. Pryce. The Hotel also has 1 mile on the Chwefru and approximately 1 mile on the Dulas which is available to hotel guests only. This water is stocked annually with brown trout.

A beautiful spring scene as the salmon angler studies a beat above Builth Wells (*John Tarlton*)

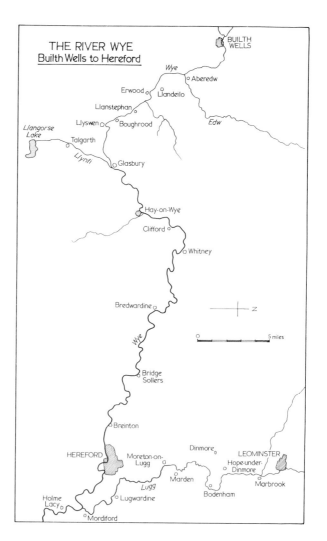

THE RIVER WYE
Builth Wells to Hereford

Beulah Mrs Copeland at The Trout Inn, can issue tickets for water on the Cammarch at the rear of the Inn plus another stretch. Access is off the main A483.

Llanwrtyd Wells Fishing permits can be obtained from the Neuadd Arms, Llanwrtyd Wells, Powys, for 300yd of both banks of the Dulas. This fishing is ¾ mile upstream of the point where it meets the Irfon to 100yd above the bridge between Cefn-gorwydd and Cynala. This hotel also issues permits for the Irfon on about ½ mile of both banks from below the level crossing upstream. There are two further 300yd stretches on the left bank and 300yd on the right bank above and below the confluence with the Dulas.

Residents only at the Abernant Lake Hotel, Llanwrtyd Wells, Powys, can fish ¾ mile of the left bank of the Irfon. This fishing extends from a point below the railway station to the boundary of Glan Irfon Farm.

Llanwrtyd Wells AA have 2,500yd of the right bank of the Irfon. This fishing is parallel to the Abergwesyn road and starts from above Cwm Irfon Bridge to a point 200yd downstream of the stepping stones 1 mile north of the road bridge. Day permits can be obtained from the Secretary, Mr P. J. Cook, The Medical Hall, Llanwrtyd Wells, Powys. This Association also has ¼ mile of both banks of the Irfon known as Penybont Farm and about ¼ mile of the right bank at Esgairmoel Uchaf. Fishing for trout is with fly, worm or spinning.

The Dol-y-Coed Hotel has 2,700yd available to hotel residents only. The fishing is from Llanwrtyd Wells to Pont Newydd and access is off the main A483. Spinning, minnow, worm and fly can be used for trout and there is no bag limit.

Abergwesyn The Llwynderw Hotel can offer fishing to guests on the upper part of the Wye system.

Builth Wells Groe Park and Irfon AC has 1½ miles of the left bank of the Irfon and ½ mile of the right bank; tickets from Mr C. Bradley, Bradleys, Builth Wells or Mrs N. Asbury, Tackle Shop, Builth Wells. Access to the fishing is from Builth Wells Car Park and Groe Car Park. Fly and worm for trout; no spinning.

Builth Wells to Hereford *(See map on page 174)*

At Builth the Wye curves to the north before continuing on its south-easterly course to Aberedw, where the Edw comes in on the right bank. The A470 is close to the Wye from Builth to Llyswen where there is a narrow suspension bridge. Below Erwood the Bach Howey comes in and then the river passes Llanstephan, Boughrood and Llyswen. Here the Wye makes a big sweep almost East and the Llynfi, out of Llangorse Lake, joins the river above Glasbury. The river now runs north-east to Hay and the valley widens out. A few miles further down we come to some more magic names of the Wye, Rhydspence, Whitney, Winforton (of record salmon fame), Bredwardine, Moccas, and Bridge Sollars and so on eastwards to Hereford. Between Whitney and Bredwardine the river meanders considerably and towards Hereford the valley widens again.

From Builth downstream the coarse-fish population starts to rise as does the average size of the trout. With some exceptions, where there are good gravel conditions, the trout fishing deteriorates as we move downstream and by the time we reach Hereford or Holme Lacy it is non-existent as a sport. You will still catch occasional fine trout but they will be heavily outnumbered by coarse fish. For trout fishing from about Hereford down you have to go to the tributaries, the Monnow being by far the best. Other good possibilities are the Lugg, Garron and Trothy.

Llanstephan The Estate Manager at Cwrt-y-Grabau, Llanstephan can offer 1 mile of single bank water on the Ithon. Fly, spinning and worm allowed, no bag limit.

Mr C. Fry, Blue Boar Hotel, Hay-on-Wye, controls 2¼ miles of left-bank fishing at Llanstephan. Available to guests for short or long periods but enquiries by letter please.

Llyswen Mr D. Watson, Bridgend Inn, owns 300yd of the Wye on the right bank, with access near the Inn. Trout up to about ¾lb can be caught with no bag limit. Spinning, fly and worm for both salmon and trout.

The Maesllwch and Llanthomas water consists of 4 miles of left bank downstream of Glasbury and this can be fished for salmon on application to Messrs Woosnam & Tyler, Estate Agents, Dolgarreg, North Road, Builth Wells.

Hay Castle and Clyro Court waters Mr W. N. Lloyd, Bridgend Cottage, Glasbury, can issue tickets for salmon fishing on both these waters. There is a 2 mile stretch of the right bank on the Hay Castle water at Hay on Wye. The Clyro Court water has 1 mile of the left bank at Hay. Access from riverside car park and by foot across fields.

The Glanwye water consists of 1 mile of right bank downstream of Hay-on-Wye. There is no bag limit for trout and salmon fishing may be arranged. For the latter, apply to Mr Potter,

Glanwye, Hay-on-Wye. Access on foot from roadside car parks. *The Moccas water*, 8½ miles of right bank at Bredwardine, can be fished for salmon and trout on application to Mr A. T. Stockwell, Red Lion Hotel, Bredwardine. Access is via riverside car parks.

Humber Mr R. Rigby, Humber Court, Humber, near Leominster, has 1 mile of trout fishing on the Humber brook which is available to resident guests. Access is from the A44 Leominster to Bromyard road, taking the Risbury road for ¾ mile then taking the Humber turning. Bag limit 3 fish. Mr G. Warren, Humber Grange, Humber, has 150yd on the Humber brook which is available to guests.

Breinton The BAA has 1¼ miles of the left bank of the Wye with salmon and trout fishing. To reach Breinton, take the Breinton road from Hereford. The BAA also has 1¼ miles of the right bank, known as the Belmont water. Salmon and trout fishing. For access, take the A49 from Hereford. Turn right at island on A465 Abergavenny road 1½ miles. Turn right at road to Eaton Bishop and right again at sign for Belmont House.

Hereford Some of the Hereford hotels can arrange salmon fishing for guests but the availability of this varies and individual enquiries will have to be made.

Messrs Herbert Hatton, 64 St Owen Street, Hereford, can usually arrange salmon fishing on various parts of the river. Contact Mr. Owen.

Bernard Thorpe & Partners, Thorpe House, Broad Street, Hereford can sometimes arrange salmon fishing.

Richard Harris & Co, 125 Eign Street, Hereford, have about 20 miles available for salmon fishing, plus a holiday cottage.

Two other estate agents who may be able to arrange salmon fishing are Woosnam & Tyler, Builth Wells, and Knight Frank & Rutley, Hereford.

Hereford to Ross-on-Wye *(See map on page 179)*

It is 16 miles from Hereford to Ross by road but more than 26 by river and there are some very large bends and loops, explained by the fact that the river falls only about 70ft over this distance. Below Hereford, the Lugg, the main tributary, joins the river and there is quite a lot of fishing available.

The Ford Bridge water, on the Lugg, consists of 1 mile of left bank and tickets can be obtained from Mr T. Helm, Ford Farm, Ford Bridge, Nr Leominster. This stretch is for trout fishing and is for guests only.

Marlbrook Mr Patrick, Marlbrook Farm, Nr Leominster has 750yd on the Lugg adjacent to the A49. Tickets from Mrs Patrick for trout fishing. Access through the farm entrance off the A49 at Marlbrook.

Dinmore The Landlord, Railway Inn, Dinmore, owns 100yd of the right bank of the Lugg off the A49 midway between Hereford and Leominster. Trout fishing with access off the main Dinmore to Bodenham road through the Inn car park.

Marden Longworth Hall Hotel has ½ mile of the Lugg and this can be fished on application to Mrs Smith, Longworth Hall, Lugwardine, but the fishing is available only with meals or accommodation. There are some trout and there is no bag limit. Take the A49 Hereford to Leominster road, turn for Marden. Go over the stile at bridge, then ¾ mile downstream.

Moreton Miss A. R. Dutson, Green Bank, Munderfield, Bromyard, has ¾ mile of right bank on the Lugg downstream of Moreton. Some trout and no bag limit. Access is off Marden to Moreton road.

Lugg Mill The Lugg Mill stretch on the Lugg consists of about 800yd of the left bank downstream of Lugg Bridge. It can be fished on application to Mrs Garlick, Lugg Bridge House, Lugwardine. There are some trout and no bag limit. Access off the A465 through yard gate into meadow.

The Rectory water on the Lugg has 300yd of the left bank immediately upstream of Mordiford Bridge. Tickets from Lady Hughes-Morgan, The Old Rectory, Mordiford. Some trout, and access from the Rectory driveway off the B4224.

Bodenham A good deal of fishing on the Lugg belongs to the BAA. The Bodenham to Sutton water consists of several miles with some gaps in between stretches. The Lugg Mill to Mordiford stretch also has several miles of fishing. There are some trout. For access to the Bodenham fishery take the A465 Hereford road from Bromyard to Burley Gate crossroads. Turn right along the A417 to Bodenham and Dinmore. For Lugg Mill take the A4103 from Worcester to Hereford direct to Lugg Mill.

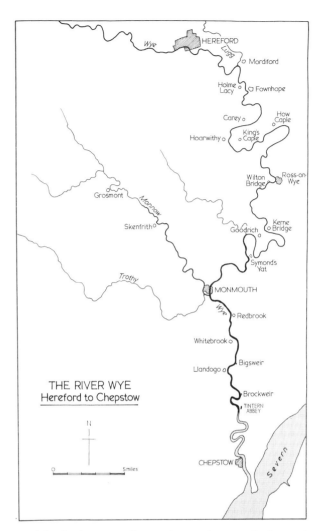

THE RIVER WYE
Hereford to Chepstow

N

0   5miles

After Mordiford, the Wye flows almost due south through wide
meadows to Fownhope, then takes a great loop eastwards under
Caplar Hill. It then turns south-west at Ballingham, in a rather
deep valley inside the loop, to be followed soon by Carey and
Hoarwithy. From Hoarwithy the river turns almost 90° to run
past Kings Caple then starts curving back almost parallel with
itself before Sellack to reach Fawley and How Caple. It then
takes an even tighter turn through open country past Hole in the
Wall before making another big loop and dropping south where
the wide valley is overlooked by Ross.

179

Wilton Bridge The BAA owns the Wilton fishery at Ross. This is ½ mile of the left bank beginning one meadow below Wilton Bridge. A few trout and salmon. Ample car parking near Wilton Bridge.

Ross-on-Wye to Chepstow *(See map on page 179)*

At Ross the river passes under the A40 at Wilton Bridge and travels in a southerly direction through open country before turning almost 90° to flow south-east again. Here the famous salmon pools, the Dog Hole and Vanstone, are to be found. The river then comes to Goodrich and the beautiful Kerne Bridge under Coppet Hill.

The Wye now takes a tight loop to skirt the hilly Forest of Dean and on to Lower Lydbrook and English Bicknor. Another great northerly loop takes the river under the world-famous view-point of Symonds Yat Rock and at the top of the loop the Garron joins the Wye.

The river flows south now to curve back past the enormous

The tidal river at Chepstow Castle (*John Tarlton*)

limestone Seven Sisters Rocks then west and south-west to take the Mally brook. Still overlooked by the Forest of Dean the Wye receives the Monnow at Monmouth itself. Just beyond Monmouth the Trothy comes in on the right bank.

Symonds Yat The BAA also has 1 mile of both banks of the Wye starting behind the cafe at Symonds Yat and extending downstream to a point above the island. Some salmon and trout. For access turn left off the A40 Monmouth road at Symonds Yat sign.

Monmouth The BAA owns another stretch consisting of about ½ mile of both banks starting at the confluence with the Mally brook and finishing downstream just above the boathouse. Some salmon and a few trout.

The Glanmonnow Estate The BAA has about ½ mile of both banks of the Monnow from Garway Mill downstream. The BAA has a half-mile stretch of left bank fishing below the mill. This extends, apart from one small stretch of private fishing, to the weir. Good trout fishing.

Grosmont Mr T. Vaughan, Tresenny Farm, Grosmont, Abergavenny, Gwent, has ¾ mile of right bank on the Monnow downstream of Grosmont Village. Access from gate opposite the farmhouse. Trout fishing, no bag limit.

Skenfrith Mr W. E. Price, Malthouse Farm, Skenfrith, Abergavenny, Gwent, has ¾ mile of left bank upstream of the farm.

The Priory water comprises 200yd of right bank on the Monnow upstream of the road at the rear of the motel. Prices from the Priory Motel, Skenfrith, Abergavenny, Gwent.

After Monmouth the river runs south-east to Redbrook after which the general course of the river is south, to Llandogo, Brockweir and Tintern. The valley here is steep and wooded and the river and road follow each other closely. Not far from Llandogo is Coed Ithel, the lowest proper salmon-fishing beat on the Wye. Below Tintern the river continues on its winding course between wooded hills to Wyndcliff and the great twist around the Lancaut peninsula brings it to Chepstow and the estuary.

19
Coarse Fish

The coarse fishing of the Wye is some of the finest in the country and there is plenty of it. Some areas, like the lower Lugg, get heavily fished and it is natural that busy areas like Hereford should have considerable demands made on the available water. Nevertheless because of the very wide distribution of all coarse fish, except roach and perch which are found more locally, virtually any area will provide good fishing. The extreme upper reaches are mostly trout waters but they have a good head of grayling. After prolonged rain it will be found that the upper river will run off more quickly and be back to normal fishing level sooner than the lower reaches.

As we move downstream from Llangurig the Wye picks up the Marteg, Ithon, Irfon, Llynfi and Lugg. The Ithon, Llynfi and Lugg can all colour the main river badly and the Lugg, the largest tributary, can raise the main river level quite a lot. It can be helpful, if you do not live close to the river, to ring the gauging station on Hereford 55333 for the pre-recorded message about conditions on the river and prospects for the next few days.

The use of maggots is banned for some months on most parts of the Wye but a recent relaxation has restricted the ban to the period between 14 March and 14 September. Previously they could not be used between 14 March and 26 October. The ban applies in the following areas:

River Wye.
River Ithon and its tributaries.
River Irfon and its tributaries.
River Marteg.
River Llynfi, downstream of Llangorse eel trap.

River Duhonw.
River Edw.
River Elan, below Caban Coch Dam.
River Trothy.

The byelaw also applies to the use of natural or artificial grubs or larvae. The Lugg and Monnow are exempt from this byelaw.

Doldowlod Starting in the upper part of the Wye, Doldowlod Estate has about 4 miles on the Wye. Pike, chub, dace and roach can be caught and information can be obtained from Mr G. Phillips, Laundry Cottage, Doldowlod, Llandrindod Wells. Also at Doldowlod, the BAA has two lengths of the left bank. One of these extends upstream from the Vulcan Arms for ¼ mile. The other begins at the disused railway bridge and extends ½ mile downstream. There is a small section of about 300yd on the right bank. The river here is fast and rocky.

Llanddewi On the Ithon, which enters the Wye below Newbridge-on-Wye, the Walsh Arms, Llanddewi, Llandrindod Wells, has one mile of both banks downstream of Llanddewi Bridge. Chub, dace and grayling are present and details can be obtained from Mr C. Daniels.

Llandegley Mr D. W. Lewis, of Aber Mithyl Farm, Llandegley, Penybont, has 1 mile of the Ithon on the left bank downstream of the farm. There is ¼ mile on the right bank downstream of the farm also. Directions from the farm which is reached by a lane from the A44 near Llandegley. Again, it is mostly chub, dace and grayling fishing.

Penybont The Severn Arms has some 3 miles of fishing on the Ithon, about 1 mile of which is adjacent to the hotel. Fishing is free to hotel guests and information can be obtained from Mr K. W. Davies.

The Brynthomas water has ¾ mile of the Ithon on the left bank downstream of Brynthomas Bridge and ¼ mile of the right bank upstream of the bridge. Chub, dace and grayling. Information from Mr Owen, Brynthomas, Penybont, Llandrindod Wells, Powys.

Cefnllys Mr W. R. Collard, Noyadd Farm, Cefnllys, Penybont, can issue tickets for 3 miles of the Ithon. This comprises 1 mile of the right bank upstream from Shaky Bridge and 2 miles of the left bank upstream from the bridge. Chub, dace and grayling.

Llanbadarn 1 mile of the left bank of the Ithon can be fished on application to Mr Harris, Great Cellws Farm, Llandrindod Wells. The water is from Llanbadarn Bridge downstream. Mostly chub and dace.

Llandrindod Wells The AA has about 5 miles of the Ithon from Llanyre Bridge to Disserth Bridge. Chub, dace and grayling, with information from C. Selwyn & Sons, 4 Park Crescent, Llandrindod Wells.

The Dolfawr water Another piece of Ithon fishing. Here there is 1½ miles of the right bank upstream of Pont ar Ithon Bridge, Newbridge-on-Wye. Information from Mr R. Tyler, Dolfawr Farm, Newbridge-on-Wye. Here again, the dominant species are chub, dace and grayling.

There are several pieces of fishing available on the Irfon, which enters the Wye from the right bank at Builth. There are reasonable numbers of coarse fish with some chub, dace, grayling and pike in this tributary although it is predominantly a trout water.

Llangammarch Wells The Cammarch Hotel has water on three rivers. There are 1¾ miles on the left bank of the Irfon between Garth and Llangammarch Wells. On the Cammarch there are two stretches. 1½ miles from Llangammarch to Llwynbrain Bridge and 1½ miles from Llwncadwgan to Blackbridge. There is also a mile of fishing on the Dulas above Llanafon weir. Tickets are available on these waters according to the number of guests staying at the hotel. Details from Mr G. Jones.

Mrs J. F. Pryce, The Lake Hotel, has 4 miles of one-bank fishing on the Irfon. Mostly chub and dace with a few pike. The fishing is available to hotel guests only. About 1 mile of the Dulas, a tributary of the Irfon, is also available. Chub, dace and grayling can be caught.

Beulah Tickets to fish at the rear of the Trout Inn and on a stretch south-west of the Inn can be obtained from Mr Copeland. This fishing is on another tributary of the Irfon, the Cammarch. Mostly chub and dace.

Llanwrtyd Wells The AA has two small stretches. The first is ¼ mile both banks at Penybont Farm, and the second ¼ mile of the right bank at Esgairmoel Uchaf. Details from Mr Cook, Medical

Hall, Victoria Square, Llanwrtyd Wells.

In an effort to provide better facilities for fishermen some of the Llanwrtyd and Llangammarch Wells hotels have joined forces and now control about 5 miles of fishing on various rivers. Details can be obtained from Mr Green, Neuadd Arms, Llanwrtyd Wells, or Mr Clark, Carlton Court on the Dol-y-Coed road, near Llanwrtyd Wells.

The Dol-y-Coed Hotel, Llanwrtyd Wells, has 2700yd from Llanwrtyd Wells to Pont Newydd. This fishing is available to hotel residents only.

The Abernant Lake Hotel, Llanwrtyd Wells, will issue tickets for about ¾ mile of the left bank downstream from the Lake to Bule Cliffs when the water is not required by hotel guests. Fishing is free to residents.

Builth Wells Groe Park and Irfon AC has 1½ miles on the left bank and ½ mile on the right bank of the Irfon and tickets can be obtained from Mr. C. Bradley, Bradleys, Builth Wells. The usual tributary coarse fish can be caught, chub, dace and grayling but no maggot fishing or spinning is allowed.

Llyswen Coming back to the main river, the Bridgend Inn has about 300yd of right-bank fishing on the Wye. Mostly chub, grayling and dace, with some pike. Spinning and worm allowed and tickets can be obtained from Mr D. Watson.

The Cwmbach Lodge water comprises 2 miles of both banks of the Llynfi, a tributary which runs out of Llangorse Lake and enters the Wye near Glasbury. Prices can be obtained from Mr W. N. Lloyd, Bridgend Cottage, Glasbury-on-Wye. There are chub, dace, perch, roach, grayling and a few pike in the stretch. Mr Lloyd can also provide information about the Ford Fawr water, 2 miles of right bank at Glasbury. Access is from the A438 at Glasbury. Most species are present and we are now in the really productive area of the Wye as far as the coarse fisherman is concerned.

Hay Castle and Clyro Court waters 40-day tickets to fish the Hay Castle water are available. This water comprises 2 miles of the right bank upstream of Hay Bridge and the tickets can be obtained from Mr R. A. Bufton, Treble Hill Cottage, Glasbury. Daylight fishing only here. Some perch in additon to the more usual coarse fish. Prices for the Hay Castle and Clyro Court waters can be obtained from Mr W. N. Lloyd, Bridgend Cottage, Glasbury-on-Wye. Clubs shold write first to c/o Mr H. Brodie-Smith, Poolpardon Cottage, Clifford, Hay-on-Wye. The Clyro Court water is 1 mile of the left bank at Hay. Perch and roach are present as well as the more usual Wye species. Daylight fishing only.

The Glanwye water has 1 mile of the right bank below Hay. 30-day tickets are issued by Mr W. Potter, Glanwye, Hay-on-Wye. There are some perch in the stretch as well as chub, dace, grayling and pike. Daylight fishing only and access is from the roadside car park on the B4350.

Whitney Mrs Williams, Gabalfa Farm, Whitney-on-Wye, can issue tickets for 1 mile on the left bank of the Wye between Whitney and Bronydd. Roach and perch as well as the usual chub, dace and pike.

The Moccas water can be fished on application to Mr A. F. Stockwell, Red Lion Hotel, Bredwardine, Hereford. There are 8½ miles of the right bank at Bredwardine and fish present are chub, dace, grayling, pike and some perch. Daylight fishing only.

Bridge Sollers Garnons Estate Office, Bridge Sollers, Hereford, will issue tickets for 2½ miles of the left bank of the Wye at Bridge Sollers Bridge. Some perch as well as the more usual Wye fish. Access is on foot from the main road with some parking at the riverside. Daylight fishing only and 100-day tickets are available.

Breinton The BAA has 1¼ miles on the left bank of the Wye and 1¼ miles of the right bank, known as the Belmont water. Most species of fish present.

Hereford The AA has about 6½ miles on the Wye. Tickets can be obtained from Messrs Herbert Hatton, 64 St Owen St, Hereford. This firm can often provide tickets for various fisheries.

The Ford Bridge water Mr T. Helm, Ford Farm, Ford Bridge, Nr Leominster, has about 1 mile on the left bank of the Lugg, the largest tributary of the Wye. Tickets can be obtained from Mrs Helm but fishing is only available to guests. Some big chub and pike in this water as well as grayling and dace.

Leominster Mrs Patrick, Marlbrook Farm, Nr Leominster can issue 10-day tickets for 750yd of the Lugg adjacent to the A49.

A winter coarse angler prepares to net yet another chub — a testimony to the superb game and coarse sport offered by the Wye

Daylight fishing only.

Dinmore 100yd of the right bank of the Lugg near the A49 midway between Hereford and Leominster are available from the landlord of the Railway Inn, Dinmore. Access is off the Dinmore to Bodenham road. Weekend tickets can be arranged.

Marden Longworth Hall Hotel has ½ mile of the Lugg. Tickets from Mrs Smith, Longworth Hall Hotel, Lugwardine. Access is from the A49 Hereford to Leominster road. Pike, chub, dace, grayling and gudgeon.

Moreton Miss A. R. Dutson issues tickets for ¾ mile of the Lugg on the right bank downstream of Moreton. Contact her at Green Bank, Munderfield, Bromyard. Most coarse fish present and access off the Marden to Moreton road.

Lugg Mill Mrs Garlick, Lugg Bridge House, Lugwardine, issues tickets for about 800yd of the left bank of the Lugg downstream from Lugg Bridge. Chub, dace, pike and grayling with access from the A465.

The Rectory water Some 300yd of the left bank of the Lugg immediately upstream of Mordiford Bridge can be fished on application to Lady Hughes-Morgan, The Old Rectory, Mordiford. Mostly chub and dace. Access via the Old Rectory drive off the B4224, with fishing during daylight only.

The Sufton water is about 1 mile, both banks, of the Wye downstream from Mordiford Bridge. Tickets from Mrs E. Boulcott, Yew Tree Cottage, Mordiford. Some roach as well as chub, dace and grayling. Fishing during daylight hours with access close to the B4224.

Fownhope Guests of Longworth Hall Hotel, Lugwardine, may obtain permission to fish the Longworth Hall stretch of 1000yd of the left bank at Fownhope. Most coarse fish and there is a further stretch available for guests during the salmon close season.

Holme Lacy Messrs Herbert Hatton, 64 St Owen Street, can issue tickets for Holme Lacy No 5 beat. This is some ¾ mile of the right bank. Most species. Access is from the roadside park.

Kings Caple Occasional tickets obtainable from Capt J. F. Cockburn, Pennoxtone Court, Kings Caple, Nr Hereford, for fishing on the Wye at Kings Caple. Chub, dace, pike and some roach.

Ross The AA has fishing on the Wye from Awkward Stile down to the Rowing Club. Tickets from G & B Sports, 19 High St, Ross-on-Wye or Dean's Fishing Shop, Broad St, Ross. Some roach and a few perch as well as chub, dace, pike and odd grayling. Access is from the coach park in Homms Road, Ross.

Ross Town water Tickets can also be obtained from G & B Sports and Dean's. This fishing is from the Rowing Club House to the island below Wilton Bridge but excluding the Hope and Anchor frontage. Chub, dace, pike and some roach.

Wilton The Wilton Fishery belongs to the BAA and extends for ½ mile on the left bank of the Wye, starting one meadow below Wilton Bridge. Usual Wye coarse fish. Access from the lay-by near Wilton Bridge. Parts of this fishing can get badly weeded during seasons of low summer water.

Symonds Yat The BAA also has 1 mile of both banks of the Wye starting behind the cafe at Symonds Yat and extending downstream to a point above the island below the Saracen's Head.

Access off the A40 Monmouth road turning left at Symonds Yat sign. Usual Wye coarse fish.

Monmouth The BAA has about ½ mile of both banks of the Wye starting at the confluence with the Mally brook and extending down to just above the boathouse. Some roach and big chub as well as dace and pike. At Monmouth the Monnow joins the Wye and there is excellent fishing in this tributary. The Monnow can get thick and red when in flood.

Skenfrith Mr W. E. Price, Malthouse Farm, Skenfrith, Abergavenny, Gwent, has ¾ mile of the Monnow on the left bank upstream of the farm in Skenfrith village. Some roach as well as chub, dace and grayling. 15-day tickets are available. Access is off the B4521 to Skenfrith road.

Grosmont Tresenny Farm, Grosmont, Abergavenny, has ¾ mile of the right bank downstream of Grosmont village. Applications to Mr Vaughan. Roach, chub, dace and grayling. Daylight only.

The Priory water consists of 200yd on the right bank of the Monnow upstream of the road at the rear of the Priory Motel, Skenfrith, Abergavenny.

Tintern Well down the Wye is the Tintern Estate Fishery with 1½ miles of both banks from Brockweir Bridge to Tintern Abbey. Tickets from Mr J. Jones, The Rock, Tintern, Chepstow. Pike, chub and dace are present but the area is tidal and low tide is reckoned to be the best time for fishing. Access is from the A466 Monmouth to Chepstow road.

It should be mentioned that in addition to this fishing other parts of the Wye can be fished from time to time. Occasional permission is given during the salmon close season for coarse fishermen to fish some of the best waters on the river but these must be ferreted out individually. A polite letter, enclosing a SAE, will sometimes do the trick but if you are lucky enough to be given permission to fish these superb coarse-fishing waters please remember what a privilege it is and act accordingly.

Hotels, guest houses, tackle shops and even estate agents in the Wye area are worth approaching for fishing. Even though they may not own rights they can often arrange a day or two for people and careful enquiries could lead you to some superb sport.

For BAA membership details write (with SAE) to The General Secretary, BAA Ltd, 40 Thorp Street, Birmingham B5 4AU.

20
Reservoirs and Lakes

No book on the Wye would be complete without mention of the reservoirs in the headwaters. Built to supply the city of Birmingham there are five main reservoirs in the valleys of the Elan and Claerwen. They are: Claerwen (650 acres), Caban Coch and Gareg ddu (500 acres), Pen-y-gareg (124 acres) and Craig Goch (217 acres). The reservoirs are now under the control of the Welsh National Water Authority and the Severn–Trent Authority.

Claerwen is by far the newest reservoir and was opened on 20 October, 1952. Pen-y-gareg, Gareg ddu and Caban Coch are lightly stocked with brown trout and Craig Goch now has a good head of American brook trout which are giving good fishing and acclimatising very well. They are easier to catch than brown trout. After 1976 no more rainbows were put in the reservoirs. Claerwen is a wild trout water.

The season is from 28 March to 30 September, except on Claerwen where the season begins on 1 March. Fishing is restricted to between half an hour before sunrise and half an hour after sunset. Permits for day, week or season fishing can be obtained from Elan Valley Estate Office, Elan Village, Rhayader, Powys.

Several boats are available. A motor boat costs £2.50 a day and a rowing boat £1 a day. There is a bag limit of 6 fish which must be not less than 10in overall. Fly only is permitted on the reservoirs but spinning, worming and fly may be used on the streams. Worming finishes on 31 August.

The Claerwen stream water is of good quality but lacking in nutrients and slightly acidic. There are few weeds. The best trout in the feeder streams are in the Claerddu which is slower than the Claerwen. There is a growing demand for reservoir fishing as pressure builds up on the rivers and the Elan reservoirs are proving popular.

A very dark or black fly seems to be best on the reservoirs and patterns like Sweeney Todd and a long-shanked Zulu are good start-of-season flies. Black Pennell, Blae and Black and Claret and Mallard are other useful flies. At the start of the season a sinking line is best to get the flies well down in the water but be careful, in some of the really deep places this could result in the flies ending up almost below you.

Long rods are popular and an 11-footer is not out of the ordinary. However, to use such a rod to its full potential you need to be a really good caster, and strong. Many ordinary fishermen would do better with a 10ft or even 9ft 6in rod which they could really make to work. Length of rod does not necessarily help you to gain increased casting distance.

Towards the end of April or early May the Elan trout will begin to rise to a dry fly. Wet fly or nymph is then best fished with a floating line which has a sinking tip. A 3yd cast is the most usual. Three flies are often used on the cast. A Zulu on the bottom, a Butcher on the bottom dropper and a Claret and Mallard on the top dropper make a sound offering for Elan trout. Claerwen probably fishes best later than the other reservoirs although it opens earlier.

In addition to the reservoirs there is quite a lot of lake and pool fishing available and the following is a selection:

Llyn Gwyn A 16 acre lake. Can be fished for trout in daylight only. Tickets from Mrs Price, Nantmynach Farm, Nantmel, Rhayader, or Mrs R. M. Powell, Garth House, Rhayader. Access, turn off the A44 at the signpost for Doldowlod, midway between Rhayader and Cross Gates. Follow lane for 1 mile then via signposted footpath through ½ mile Forestry Commission woodlands to the lake. Fly only and there is a bag limit of 6 brown and 6 rainbows. Size limit, rainbows 10in, browns 8in.
Llandrindod Wells Lake 16½ acres. Tickets can be obtained from J. R. Chapman, The Lake, Princess Avenue, Llandrindod Wells. The lake is well signposted from Llandrindod. Tench, bream, roach and carp are present as well as gudgeon.
Troedyrhiw Lakes 1¾ and ¾ acre each. Can be fished for trout. Tickets from Mr Whelan, Troedyrhiw isaf, Llangammarch Wells. Access above the village of Llangammarch Wells about 12

miles from Llandovery to the south and Builth Wells to the north. Brown trout and rainbows with a bag limit of 2 fish.

The Dderw Pools Offer good carp fishing. Tickets can be obtained from Mr D. Eckley, Dderw Farm, Nr Llyswen, Powys.

Llangorse Lake The largest lake in the area which covers some 400 acres. Fishing is free but best from a boat, which can be hired. Roach, perch, pike, bream and eels present and access is from the A40 or B4560.

Newbrook Pool Covers 1 acre and has brown and rainbow trout and a 3-fish limit. Fly only with tickets from Mr Griffiths, Newbrook Farm, Wormbridge, Hereford and Worcester.

Hindwell Pool Covers 6 acres and tickets are available from Mr H. Price, Hindwell, Walton, Presteigne, Powys. Brown and rainbows.

Flintsham Pool Offers coarse fishing for pike, perch and roach with tickets from Mr J. M. Jones, Flintsham Lodge, Titley, Kington.

Milton Pool Has carp. Permission to fish from Mr. E. Morris, Milton Farm, Pembridge, Hereford and Worcester.

Nicholson Farm Lake Covers 2 acres with fishing for brown trout and rainbows. Tickets from Mrs Brooke, Upper Nicholson, Docklow, Nr Leominster. Access, farm drive signposted as Docklow.

West End Farm Lake About 2 acres with coarse fishing for roach, tench, carp and bream. Tickets from Mr Bozward, West End Farm, Docklow, Nr Leominster.

Tillington Court Lakes Two small lakes of 1 acre and ¼ acre with brown trout and carp. Prices on application to Mr R. P. Powell, Tillington Court, Farm, Tillington, Hereford and Worcester. Access is by the farm roadway off the Tillington to Canon Pyon road.